PRAISE

"*Me Too* is a great reminder of how wonderful the Father's love is for us—even in a world of pain and suffering. Thank you, Jon Weece, for giving us a glimpse of what Heaven will be like."

—MARK BATTERSON, *NEW YORK TIMES* BESTSELLING
AUTHOR OF *THE CIRCLE MAKER* AND LEAD PASTOR
OF NATIONAL COMMUNITY CHURCH

"*Me Too* is a message that Jon Weece taught me long before writing this book. He will help you see that you are not alone. God is with you, he understands what you are going through, and it's safe to be vulnerable and ask for his help."

—KYLE IDLEMAN, BESTSELLING AUTHOR OF *NOT A FAN*
AND PASTOR AT SOUTHEAST CHRISTIAN CHURCH

"Looking back over my years as a radio host, I can name a handful of guests that have so deeply impacted me that I find myself still thinking about those conversations long after the interview is over. Jon Weece is one such guest. And I didn't see him coming. His humility and self-deprecating humor disarmed me. His Kingdom heart undid me. Even so, I've tried to identify how and why he—out of hundreds of interviews—stood out to me. I think it's because he loves people like Jesus did and does. If you long to be comfortable in your own skin—just the way God made you, and if you desire to be at home with the love of Jesus in a way that heals you, and if you're willing to see that same love transform the world around you, you've come to the right place. May Jesus himself meet you on the pages of Jon's excellent new book, *Me Too*. Whatever you've experienced of God's love, know this: he has more for you."

—SUSIE LARSON, TALK RADIO HOST, NATIONAL
SPEAKER, AND AUTHOR OF *YOUR SACRED YES*

ME
TOO

ME
TOO

EXPERIENCE THE GOD
WHO UNDERSTANDS

JON WEECE

NELSON
BOOKS

An Imprint of Thomas Nelson

Published in Nashville, Tennessee, by Nelson Books, an imprint of Thomas Nelson. Nelson Books and Thomas Nelson are registered trademarks of HarperCollins Christian Publishing, Inc.

The author is represented by the literary agency of The Gates Group, 1403 Walnut Lane, Louisville, Kentucky 40223.

Interior designed by James A. Phinney.

Thomas Nelson titles may be purchased in bulk for educational, business, fund-raising, or sales promotional use. For information, please e-mail SpecialMarkets@ThomasNelson.com.

Any Internet addresses, phone numbers, or company or product information printed in this book are offered as a resource and are not intended in any way to be or to imply an endorsement by Thomas Nelson, nor does Thomas Nelson vouch for the existence, content, or services of these sites, phone numbers, companies, or products beyond the life of this book.

Unless otherwise noted, Scripture quotations are taken from THE NEW KING JAMES VERSION. © 1982 by Thomas Nelson, Inc. Used by permission. All rights reserved.

Scriptures marked NLT are taken from the Holy Bible, New Living Translation. © 1996. Used by permission of Tyndale House Publishers, Inc., Wheaton, Illinois 60189. All rights reserved.

Scriptures marked NIV are taken from the Holy Bible, New International Version®, NIV®. Copyright © 1973, 1978, 1984, 2011 by Biblica, Inc.™ Used by permission of Zondervan. All rights reserved worldwide. www.zondervan.com.

Scriptures marked TLB are taken from The Living Bible. © 1971. Used by permission of Tyndale House Publishers, Inc., Wheaton, Illinois 60189. All rights reserved.

Scriptures marked PHILLIPS are taken from J. B. Phillips: THE NEW TESTAMENT IN MODERN ENGLISH, Revised Edition. © J. B. Phillips 1958, 1960, 1972. Used by permission of Macmillan Publishing Co., Inc.

Scriptures marked MSG are taken from The Message by Eugene H. Peterson. © 1993, 1994, 1995, 1996, 2000. Used by permission of NavPress Publishing Group. All rights reserved.

Certain names and details have been changed to protect privacy. Permission has been granted for use of real names, stories, and correspondence with some individuals.

ISBN: 978-1-4002-0693-3 (e-book)

Library of Congress Cataloging-in-Publication Data

Weece, Jon.
Me too : experience the God who understands / Jon Weece.
  pages cm
Includes bibliographical references.
ISBN 978-1-4002-0692-6
1. Christian life. I. Title.
BV4501.3.W39845 2016
248.4--dc23
  2015027221

Printed in the United States of America

16 17 18 19 20 RRD 6 5 4 3 2 1

To Ava & Silas—
God loves you. God died for you. God will never leave you. God knows you. God is for you. God lives in you. God sees you. God hears you. God will guide you. God will protect you. God will discipline you. God will challenge you. God collects your tears in a bottle. God has written your name on his hand. God knows how long you will live. God will not tempt you. God will forgive you. God will speak to you. God will defend you. God runs to you. God sings over you. God enjoys you. God is preparing a place for you. God is coming to get you. God will spend eternity with you. God will be a better Father to you than me. You can trust God with your life.

CONTENTS

CONTENTS

BEGIN HERE—ALL OF US ARE LIKE THE REST OF US

WHEN I WAS GROWING UP, MY PARENTS HAD A RECORD PLAYER AND I HAD a record filled with famous nursery rhymes. As the needle moved across the vinyl, I would hear a man with a British accent say, "Humpty Dumpty sat on a wall, Humpty Dumpty had a great fall. All the king's horses and all the king's men couldn't put Humpty together again."

The Bible doesn't use the name Humpty Dumpty, but it does say that one thing all of us have in common is all of us have fallen: "for *all* have sinned and fall short of the glory of God" (Rom. 3:23, emphasis mine). It doesn't say "some have fallen" or "a few have fallen."

All of us have fallen. *All* of us have sinned.

And if you've ever tried to pick up the shattered and scattered pieces of your life and put yourself back together again, you've come to realize it's an impossible task. When divorce divides your family, when a loved one commits suicide, when cancer claims a close friend, when you lose your job, it's easy to lose perspective. It's easier to feel broken than it is to feel put back together again.

My daughter's friend recently spent the night, and they were sitting on the couch eating ice cream and giggling. I heard Ava say to her friend, "Do you like firecrackers?"

"No, I'm afraid of firecrackers!" her friend replied with great animation.

"Me too!" Ava said with excitement. As middle school girls do, they screamed and hugged each other! They went back and forth asking each other questions, and I bet I heard the phrase "*Me too!*" a hundred times in five minutes.

C. S. Lewis once wrote, "Friendship, I have said, is born at the moment when one man says to another 'What! You too? I thought that no one but myself . . .'"[1]

I can say, "Republican or Democrat," and we won't all agree. I can say, "Tom Brady or Peyton Manning," or, "rock, rap, or country," and we won't all agree. But if I ask, "Have you made at least one decision in your life that you wish you could take back?" my guess is you would nod your head.

Sin is a universal "me too." *All* have sinned and *all* have fallen. Because all of us have sinned, all of us need a Savior. All of us are like the rest of us.

All of us are struggling. We don't like what sin has done to us and everyone around us. We don't like fear, sadness, or the pressure we feel to fit in or stand out. We don't like tension in our marriages or worrying about our finances. We don't like war and corruption and abuse and terrorism.

And what we don't like, God likes even less.

We are far from Eden. Perfection is a distant land, and paradise has been lost. Will we ever experience Eden again?

This is going to sound strange, but one of the most beautiful places to visit in Lexington is a cemetery. Weeping willows and cherry blossoms and dogwoods bend and bloom and keep watch over two-hundred-year-old gravestones.

My friends buried their son there. My wife buried her mom there.

It is a place that generates conflicting emotions because the beauty of what is aboveground collides with the ugliness of all that is belowground. Life and death are separated by nothing more than a layer of dirt.

Several times a year I stand on that dirt and help people try to make sense of why they have to say good-bye to their loved ones. No matter how old the deceased person is, and no matter how they died, I usually say the same thing.

"God is life. God is not death."

God is the author of life. God is the Creator of life. God is the giver of life. God is the sustainer of life. God is the redeemer of life.

God hates death more than we do. He is bothered by the pain, the separation, the questions, and the confusion that death creates. God did not design death. He designed a place called Eden to be the epicenter of his life with humanity.

Eden is where God wanted to live. Eden is where God wants to live. Eden is where God will live. And God will live there with us. We know it as heaven.

I am tired today. Really tired. I want to write in the middle of the fatigue. I want to write while I'm surrounded by exhaustion on all sides. My prayer is not for the exhaustion to go away. My prayer is that it helps me relate and understand other people's challenges. Preaching. Leading. Writing. Counseling. Parenting. Sin. These and many other challenges are contributing to my depletion. I sleep but never feel rested.

Heaven doesn't seem real to me today. A place of eternal rest sounds incredible, but I'm not there. I'm here. I'm living in a former paradise, in a fallen and flawed version of Eden. I feel so far from heaven.

The news this morning reported that two hundred girls were kidnapped from their school in Nigeria, and they are going to be sold into slavery if someone doesn't do something. The cameramen kept panning the crowd outside the school, showing the panicked and distraught faces of the moms and dads, and it's all I can do to keep it together. It's gut-wrenching because it's real.

Little girls are being held captive by men with machine guns. That should never happen, but it does. Like a boat untied from a dock, our world seems to drift farther and farther away from God. Eden seems like nothing more than a dot on the horizon of a vast ocean.

Where is God? Why does he allow little girls to be kidnapped? Why doesn't he stop it from happening? Each question is common and valid, but questions are easier to ask than answers are to find.

Pain is the common language of the human experience. Most people I know are fluent in suffering. They speak it, but they don't understand it. One of the ways people begin to heal is to sit across the table from someone who can say, "Me too."

Too many people suffer alone. And most people who suffer alone aren't looking for answers. Most people who suffer alone are looking for a friend—a friend who understands.

"Me too" friends don't need to talk. There is power in presence. There is power in just being there.

Listening may be the greatest form of love, and at the same time the most neglected form of love. People need us to notice them and to listen to them.

"Rejoice with those who rejoice, and weep with those who weep" (Rom. 12:15). The first half of that verse is easier to live out than the second half. This is true because "weeping with" requires vulnerability. Many people want intimacy. Few people understand that intimacy requires vulnerability.

Our enemy has convinced us that no one is like us. He has sold us a bag of lies that say the pain we are experiencing is unique to us. So we keep our suffering a secret. Satan wants us to suffer alone.

"Loneliness is the leprosy of modern society," Mother Teresa once wrote. I agree.

When we suffer alone, we die, but Jesus came to suffer with us and suffer for us. He died so we could live. He came to remove pain by removing sin.

The cross is God's "me too" statement to a world saturated with suffering. And the church was designed to be a "me too" community where people could suffer together. And heaven?

"God will wipe away every tear from their eyes; there shall be no more death, nor sorrow, nor crying" (Rev. 21:4). Those are the words used to describe a paradise that is void of pain.

We can look back to a cross to see that God did something about the suffering we see around us. We can look to the church and see that God is doing something about the suffering we see around us. And we can look forward to heaven to see that ultimately God will end all suffering.

BEGIN HERE—ALL OF US ARE LIKE THE REST OF US

When my daughter was two years old, I took her to Fazoli's for lunch. She walked out with a free balloon and a belly full of breadsticks. That night we were playing in her bedroom, and I took her balloon by the string to tie it to the edge of her bed. As I did, the balloon rubbed against the textured ceiling and popped. Her bottom lip came out and a big tear streamed down her cheek, and I'll never forget it as long as I live. She said, "Daddy, you popped my balloon."

She blamed me for her pain. So I scooped her up, strapped her in her car seat, drove her to Toys"R"Us, and bought her an entire kitchen set complete with pots and pans and fake food.

A free balloon ended up costing me fifty bucks!

We have a Father who paid a high price to rid the world of suffering—suffering he didn't create and suffering he didn't cause. Suffering that breaks his heart.

And he did it because he loves us. I don't know a dad who wants to see his kids suffer.

And that's what this book is about: an eternal Father who specializes in wiping away tears, and the people he uses to help him.

PART 1

THE CROSS—
WHAT JESUS DID

I GREW UP IN A LOVING HOME. MY PARENTS WERE NOT RICH IN MONEY, BUT they were rich in love, so most of my insecurities are not worth blaming on them.

I was and still am a tall and skinny guy. I have a long neck and a funny-shaped head. It's almost as if God attached a battery pack to the back of my skull. I never would have thought anything of it until a kid at church pointed it out.

"You have a funny-shaped head," he said with a disgusted look on his face.

"It's better than having a funny-looking face," I said back.

1

Humor was my defense mechanism as a kid. If a situation made me nervous or if I didn't like the attention being paid to me, I would redirect it with sarcasm.

That boy's comment led me down a path of noticing things about myself that I had never noticed before. I wasn't fast and other boys were. I wasn't strong and other boys were. I wasn't smart and other boys were. I spent countless hours and years covering up what I was afraid others would discover about me. I spent more time thinking about what I *wasn't* in comparison to what other people *were*. I wore shirts with collars so my neck wouldn't seem so long. I got sunburned so my skin would dry out, and I wouldn't have as many pimples on my face. I wore a baseball hat to cover up the shape of my head.

There is something about the cross that helped me get comfortable in my own skin. Jesus was killed in front of a crowd of people. They had a front-row seat to his execution, which means they watched him suffer.

Jesus couldn't hide anything from the crowd, and he didn't need to. Jesus lived and died with nothing to hide.

That gives me hope. I can live and die without needing to hide anything from anyone.

The cross is a lot like this page, in that it's an interlude: a break in the rhythm and pattern of the story. God broke into humanity and planted a piece of wood in the ground to remind all of us that we don't have to stay the way we are. With your permission, that's what we're going to explore in these next chapters.

VULNERABILITY: A THREE-LEGGED RACE

WHEN I WAS YOUNGER, THERE WAS A BULLY AT MY SCHOOL WHO USED HIS size to intimidate everyone he encountered. He would frog me on the arm, sending what little amount of muscle I had into terrible spasms.

I used to pray that God would send Rocky Balboa to beat up the bully.

"God, forget the Russians," I would implore. "I need Sylvester Stallone to get in the ring with Ashley Tucker!"

Yep, the bully's name was Ashley. I was getting beat up by a boy with a girl's name! That made the torture even more unbearable.

On the playground at Rockbridge Elementary were two small hills with monkey bars spanning the gap between them. Beneath the monkey bars were tires that were supposed to serve as padding in case we fell. I never considered tires to be soft, but obviously someone else did.

One day Ashley decided to try his luck at climbing across the monkey bars. Halfway across, his luck ran out. "Please, somebody help me!" is what I remember hearing as I stood in line to play tetherball.

Ashley had pummeled so many kids that no one responded; no one ran to his rescue. We all just stood there, watching him hold on for dear life—legs flailing wildly, with a panicked look on his face. And that's when it happened.

All eyes watched as Scott Graham cautiously made his way from the basketball court to the monkey bars. Scott was from a great family and was loved by everyone in our class, so no one was too surprised that he was going to play the part of the good Samaritan in this unfolding drama.

But Scott had different plans that day.

Scott had watched Ashley rule the bathrooms and the hallways and the bus stops with an iron fist. Scott was acting on behalf of every other scrawny kid in school when he reached up, took hold of Ashley's sweatpants and underwear, pulled them down around his ankles, and walked off.

Girls gasped and covered their mouths. Boys raised their arms in the air and cheered as Ashley hung there, in all his chubby glory.

Scott's parents got a phone call from Mr. Calhoun, the principal, but Scott didn't mind the punishment because he had achieved hero status among his peers. Had we been allowed to throw a ticker-tape parade to celebrate the downfall of the great dictator, we would have hoisted Scott up onto our shoulders and marched him around the playground.

Scott became more than a legend that day. He became my friend.

Jesus had friends. He frequently stayed in the home of his good friend Peter. Houses in Capernaum were typically two-story square boxes with open courtyards in the center. What covered the courtyard was a mixture of sticks and grass and fabric that kept rain out but allowed cool air in.

Jesus had been teaching for days, so the house was packed with people. It was a once-in-a-lifetime, standing-room-only situation. Scalpers were selling tickets outside, and Mark gave us this descriptive detail in the narrative: "Four men arrived carrying a paralyzed man on a mat" (Mark 2:3 NLT).

We don't know if the man was born paralyzed or if he fell and broke his neck. We don't know if he was a single man or a married man. What we do know is that he had four friends who carried him. Four friends who loved him.

"They couldn't bring him to Jesus because of the crowd, so they dug a hole through the roof above his head. Then they lowered the man on his mat, right down in front of Jesus" (Mark 2:4 NLT).

Not even a kid could have squeezed between the people jammed into this room! This man's friends cut a hole in the roof of a stranger's house so their friend could gain a hearing with Jesus. I have some good friends in my life, but I'm not sure any of them would crank up their chain saws and ruin someone's roof for me!

There is a thread of empathy in this story. This man's friends put themselves on his mat and wondered, "What if that were me? What if I were paralyzed? What if I couldn't walk, if I had to beg to survive—what would I want my friends to do for me?"

This is a "me too" story, and it's in the Bible because Jesus was God's visible version of "me too." Every pain you've ever experienced or been through in your life, God can say, "Me too." Betrayal, misunderstanding, confusion, heartache, suffering, physical pain, fatigue, hunger, you name it—Jesus understands. Jesus can look at any situation in anyone's life and say, "Me too."

What I've learned from the four men who cut a hole in a roof for a friend is this: Everybody needs somebody. That is at the heart of living a "me too" life and building a "me too" culture.

"As a rough rule of thumb, if you belong to no groups but decide to join one, you cut your risk of dying over the next year *in half*," wrote social researcher Robert Putnam. "The single most common finding from a half century's research on the correlates of life satisfaction, not only in the United States but around the world, is that happiness is best predicted by the breadth and depth of one's social connections."[1]

I can't imagine anyone not being interested in cutting their risk of dying *in half*!

I have a friend who loves to run. Over lunch he told me about a man who finished the Boston Marathon in two hours and another man who finished in seventeen hours. It would take me a week to finish that race!

The second man has muscular dystrophy, but he completed every mile of the 26.2-mile race. Even though the winner of the race finished fifteen hours before him, the man with muscular dystrophy never gave up. And at the end of the race he paid tribute to the two people who walked beside him the entire way. Two people who never left his side. Two healthy people who have put themselves in his shoes and have come to realize that everyone needs someone. Who is that someone in your life?

Who would walk with you through death's valley? Who would carry you across the finish line when your legs give out?

Can I suggest someone to you? His name is Jesus.

And the reason you need him as a friend is because Jesus is God. I have a lot of friends, but none of them can make that claim. And some people struggle with the idea of a man being God.

"For in Christ all the fullness of the Deity lives in bodily form" (Col. 2:9 NIV).

If Olympic gold medalist Usain Bolt entered a three-legged race—running with one leg tied to a partner's leg—it wouldn't diminish his innate running ability or change his status as the world's fastest sprinter. But he would be voluntarily limiting the use of his abilities. Likewise, Jesus' status as fully God was not diminished in the incarnation.

"The incarnation was more an addition of human attributes than a loss of divine attributes," noted theologian Millard Erickson.[2]

Jesus was God's primary response to the pain we see in the world around us and the pain we experience in our own lives. He didn't send a bouquet of flowers and a greeting card. God sent his Son. He entered this world the way we entered this world—crying. And he left the world the way we'll leave the world—dying.

But he didn't stay dead. And that's what separates him from any other friends you have.

The kind of people you surround yourself with will determine the kind of person you become. Buzz had Woody. Laverne had Shirley. Bert had Ernie. Batman had Robin. And Bonnie had Clyde.

"Jon, you can't live the right life with the wrong friends," my parents used to tell me. Maybe you've heard the old adage: "Show me your friends and I will show you your future." Friends matter.

Jesus had friends. He ate with prostitutes, which makes religious people squirm. It makes me smile! I can see Jesus leaning over and saying to the prostitute seated next to him, "Hey, you gotta try these mashed potatoes! Go on, take some off my plate."

When religious people saw Jesus eating with prostitutes, they said, "Why does (he) eat with such scum?" (Matt. 9:11 NLT). The people the world called scum, Jesus called friends. And that includes you and me.

Years ago I went to New York City to talk to a wise friend. He's not just smart; he's experienced. Paul has lived. I sat in a comfortable chair in his office and unloaded the uncomfortable tension in my heart.

"I'm so tired I can't see straight or think straight," I said. "Physically, emotionally, and spiritually, I have nothing left to give. I just feel like quitting."

Paul didn't say anything. He just leaned in. And for the next four hours I dumped all the debris that had piled up in my heart and mind over the years. I talked about the stuff I couldn't talk about with other people. And Paul didn't try to solve any of my problems or tell me that I was wrong or that I needed to see things differently.

No, Paul listened to me.

And at the end of the four hours I took a deep breath, and we just stared at each other for a brief moment. Then Paul smiled and broke the silence with, "Let's eat! Food makes everything better!"

So we walked a few blocks to a dimly lit restaurant, and over a rib eye and a glass of sweet tea, Paul poured his wisdom into my empty heart.

We impress people with our strength, but we connect with our weakness. When we open up and admit that we need help, we run the risk of being hurt. But if we don't open up and admit that we need help, we run a greater risk of not being helped.

Vulnerability is the key to intimacy, and all of us need to experience intimacy. It's at the heart of every great friendship. I think some people are afraid to open up because they fear it will make them appear weak to their friends. But I'm convinced that we don't really have friends until we open up to people. Vulnerability strengthens any and all relationships that it flows out of.

I've noticed this dangerous trend between the genders: Many men struggle with the idolatry of independence, while many women struggle with the idolatry of dependence. Many men think they can live without anyone, whereas many women think they can't live without anyone.

We need each other, but we need Jesus even more. The closer we get to Jesus, the closer we can get to one another. So take some time today to get closer to Jesus. And if you need help, ask a friend to help you. Your vulnerability will strengthen you both.

2

ACCESSIBILITY: LUCILLE

I'M FRUSTRATED AND I DON'T KNOW WHY," RON SAID, LEANING FORWARD IN his chair. He owns his own business, and the stress of his life recently reached a boiling point.

"I feel like I'm hiding from my family," he admitted. "I love them, but everything they say and do gets on my nerves and I snap. And after I yell, after I lose my temper, I feel horrible."

"Why are you so stressed out?" I asked.

"I don't like my job. Actually, I hate my job," he said as he shook his head in frustration. "The only reason I haven't quit is because I can't afford to. I owe the bank too much money and I've created a lifestyle that my family is used to now. I'm afraid I'm losing my mind. I'm afraid I'm going to do something stupid. Tell me what to do and I'll do it. I just can't keep living like this."

I hear it a lot. Pressure.

My mom has a teapot that whistles once the water reaches a boiling point. The lid pops open and a screeching sound follows the steam that shoots out.

People don't have lids, but we do have hearts. And our hearts can only take so much pressure. Final exams. Tax season. Tryouts. Deadlines.

Burned-out. Stressed-out. Freaked-out. Worn-out. How do we dig out of the hole we find ourselves in?

During the summer of 1994, I worked the third shift in a factory that made heaters for hot water tanks. My job on the assembly line was to connect a little piece of copper wire to the back of each heater using a propane blowtorch. For eight hours every night, I stood in the same place doing the same thing and was paid minimum wage to singe the hair off my arms!

I should never be in charge of anything that has fire coming out of it.

When you work on an assembly line, you have no choice but to get to know the people working beside you, simply because of their proximity. To my right was one of the funniest people I've ever worked with. Her name was Lucille.

ACCESSIBILITY: LUCILLE

Lucille and I hit it off from day one. She was a large, gregarious, middle-aged woman who had a resounding, full-body laugh that was contagious. She kissed me on the cheek at the beginning of each shift and said, "How's my little baby doin' tonight?"

"Skinny as ever," was my standard response.

We became such good friends that she and her husband had me over for breakfast when our shift ended. I loved Lucille.

But Ray? Ray wasn't as easy to love.

Ray stood on the other side of me and smelled like a mixture of diesel fuel, sweat, Bud Light, and Old Spice aftershave. I'm guessing he was in his midseventies, and he couldn't have been more than five feet two inches tall. Soaking wet he might have weighed a hundred pounds. And for some reason, Ray didn't like me.

Every so often and out of the blue, with more chewing tobacco in his mouth than teeth, he would snarl and say to me, "Boy, one of these days, I'm going to take you out back and whoop you!"

I tried to connect with him by talking about the next monster truck show or tractor pull at the fairgrounds, but he wouldn't budge. He had made up his mind about me. Ray didn't like anything about me.

But every time Ray threatened me, Lucille would lean over, shake her finger at him, and say, "You touch this boy and I will turn you inside out!" I really don't know what that means, but if anyone could turn another human being inside out, it would be Lucille!

I don't know why Ray was so angry, but I've dealt with enough angry people in my life to know that most of them are wounded. Someone probably hurt Ray in the past. Someone who was supposed to hug him probably slugged him. Ray's anger boiled over. There's no way to keep that much anger inside.

What's the old line? "Hurt people hurt people."

Ray was feeling what Ron was feeling. Pressure.

Ron dealt with it by buying sports cars. Ray dealt with it by threatening people like me. We deal with pressure in different ways, but what we all have in common is that we all feel pressure.

Think about the pressure Jesus felt. He had to save the world. He had to solve a problem he didn't create, and the solution to the problem involved him dying. Jesus was so stressed out about saving the world that he sweat drops of blood. The medical diagnosis for this is hematidrosis. It happens when a person is so overwhelmed from a crisis that the capillaries in the forehead burst. Blood mixes with water in the sweat glands and is released through pores in the skin.

Jesus didn't want to suffer, and who could blame him? He knew what a crucifixion entailed, the brutality it involved. And he knew there was no one who could or would take his place. One friend had already betrayed him, and the other eleven friends he had were sound asleep.

So what did Jesus do when pressure had him by the throat? He prayed, "Father, if possible, remove this cup from me."

Pressure leads us to believe that everything is impossible. We won't know what is possible until we ask God for help.

When I was four years old, President Jimmy Carter visited my hometown. My dad put me on his shoulders so I could see the leader of the free world board Air Force One. A few years later, when President Ronald Reagan drove through the downtown district where I grew up, I stood on my tiptoes to see him pass by. When I was in high school, a buddy of mine and I learned that President George Bush was coming to town, so we stood on the edge of a local highway with a banner we had made. For some reason, the Secret Service didn't ask us to leave, and when the motorcade passed, President Bush leaned forward in his limousine and gave the two of us a thumbs-up. It was worth the sunburn we received while waiting!

And after Hurricane Katrina devastated New Orleans, I was invited to the White House with other pastors to discuss rebuilding plans with President George W. Bush. After passing through two security checkpoints, we were ushered into a room where the most powerful man in the world sat fifteen feet away from an ordinary man like me. The minute I sat down, I decided not to say a word unless called upon. But the pastor sitting across from me decided to do just the opposite.

He started talking and didn't stop. I was not thinking, *Love thy neighbor.* I was thinking, *Beat thy neighbor.* He talked so much we didn't get to hear what the president had to say.

Every morning I have an appointment with someone far more powerful than the president. I close my office door early in the morning—and before I turn on my phone or computer, before I pick up a book or look at my schedule, I sit in a chair and don't say anything.

I invite the God of the universe to speak to me.

Those ten minutes of silence do more for me than anything else I do in the course of a day. In the midst of all the voices that clamor for my attention, hearing the voice of God centers me and calms me.

God is a dad who loves to speak to his children. He's also a dad who loves to hear his children speak to him.

Throughout the Gospels Jesus refers to God as Abba—an Aramaic word meaning Dad. And Jesus invites us to refer to him that way too.

Joachim Jeremias wrote,

> I have examined the prayer literature of ancient Judaism, and the result of this examination was, that in no place in this immense literature is this invocation of God as "*Abba, Father,*" to be found. *Abba* was an everyday word. It

was a homely family-word. No Jew would have dared to address God in this manner, yet Jesus did it always in all his prayers which are handed down to us . . . In the Lord's prayer, Jesus authorizes his disciples to repeat the word *Abba* after him. He gives them a share in his sonship. He empowers his disciples to speak with their heavenly father in such a familiar and trusting way.[1]

Above God's fireplace is a family portrait, and if you look closely, you will see yourself in it. God came down off the throne and has pulled up a chair next to you. And with his arm around you, he's saying, "Keep on asking, and you will receive what you ask for. Keep on seeking, and you will find. Keep on knocking, and the door will be opened" (Matt. 7:7 NLT).

When my kids persistently pester me to buy something, I usually say, "If you keep asking, I'm not going to get it for you!" But God invites us to ask and keep asking. He's not bothered by our requests. He's flattered by them. And he wants to replace the pressure you're carrying around with peace.

Pressure for peace. Who wouldn't want that? Who wouldn't ask for that?

Ruth and Verena Cady shared a life as twin sisters. They shared a room, a bed, a bike, a birthday, and the same womb. What separated them from most twins is they also shared the same heart. Their bodies were fused together at the sternum, and though they had different personalities, their lives were sustained by the same three-chambered heart.

Since separation was not an option for them, cooperation became an obligation.

For their seven years of life, they did everything with the other person in mind. They ate together, ran together, studied together, danced together, and when one of them sat in the corner, the other one did too. Through good and bad, highs and lows, ups and downs, the Cady sisters were inseparable.[2]

The Bible teaches that nothing can separate us from the love of God that is in Christ Jesus.

I want to think what Jesus thinks. I want to feel what Jesus feels. I want to do what Jesus does. I want my life to mirror and mimic the life of Jesus. Prayer makes that possible.

Every night after we put our kids to bed, Allison and I have a scheduled time to talk. Over the years I've noticed it does two things for us: it guards intimacy and it grows intimacy. When communication breaks down, the relationship breaks down. If we want to share the heart of the Father, we need to have heart-to-heart conversations on a regular basis.

When I feel pressure, it's because I'm not guarding and growing the intimacy in my relationship with God through intimate conversation. When I feel pressure, it's because I'm not letting God know what's in my heart and he's not letting me know what's in his.

The marketing slogan for my cell phone says I have "anytime, anywhere minutes" at my disposal. The same can be said for my relationship with God. While I'm brushing my teeth, mowing the yard, or driving to work, I have an "anytime, anywhere" arrangement with a Father who wants to know what's going on in my heart. And he wants to let me know what's going on in his too.

When my daughter was ten years old, she wrote this paragraph about prayer in a creative writing exercise at school:

> Dear New Believer,
>
> You can pray any time you want. You can pray in church, at the store, or you can pray standing up or sitting down. You can even pray while standing on your head! Praying is like talking to a friend, but you're actually talking to God. God will listen to your prayers no matter what. You can pray a short prayer or a long prayer. God will not always answer your prayer with a "yes." He might answer with a "no" or a "wait" or a "maybe." You never know what he's gonna say, but he will say something.
>
> I hope this answers some of your questions about prayer.
>
> Your friend,
>
> Ava

I need to send that letter to my friends Ron and Ray. They need to know that they have a Father who wants to hear their voices—a Father who wants them to hear his voice.

Twenty-seven years ago, Christopher Knight walked away from his everyday life to live deep in the woods of Maine. The only time he used his voice in that lengthy period of time was when he crossed paths with a hiker and said, "Hi." Outside of that exchange, that was the only word he said or heard in twenty-seven years.[3]

God wants to talk to you, and my guess is you need to talk to him.

Pressure for peace.

ABILITY: GIVE ME YOUR LUNCH MONEY

MY ENTIRE LIFE I'VE STRUGGLED WITH FEAR.

When I was five years of age, I saw two grown men in my neighborhood get into a fistfight. It rocked my sense of security because adults weren't supposed to act like kids.

A few years later, the man who initiated the fight got drunk and spit on a boy as the boy rode past the man's driveway on his bike. I was playing basketball in my driveway when it happened, and my dad was mowing our yard. I remember hearing my dad's voice and watching him run toward the boy.

Even though my dad was a big man, it paralyzed me because I was terrified that he would get in a fight with the man. I remember running inside and hiding behind the washer and dryer in the laundry room. Later that evening when my dad came in for dinner, I emerged from my hiding place to discover that his nose was still straight and he still had all of his teeth. My dad protected the boy and eventually helped our neighbor deal with his anger issues. But the anxiety I felt that day wasn't momentary.

I went to an inner-city middle school and had a front row seat to all kinds of violence. As a result, I had bad dreams and spent several nights trying to fall asleep on the floor of my parents' bedroom.

Few places and few people felt safe once fear had wrapped itself around my heart like a boa constrictor. It choked out any courage in me and kept me from ever wanting to get up in front of a crowd. I was petrified of public speaking. It also kept me from resolving conflict in my friendships, so I avoided conflict at all costs.

Today, fear keeps me from getting close to people. I've yet to get to the bottom of it, but trust is a huge issue for me. I get suspicious of people, and I find myself putting up barriers and walls and only letting a select few ever get to know the real me. It's not fun to admit this, but it's true.

I pull people close only to push them far away.

And my guess is I'm not alone. My guess is there are others who would say their lives have been adversely affected by fear. My guess is there are others who could look at my life and say about their own lives, "Me too."

I have a friend who was teased during her teenage years for having acne. People on the bus and in the school hallway called her all kinds of cruel names and stared at her as if she carried an airborne and highly contagious disease. No one wanted to sit by her in the cafeteria, and she was never invited to slumber parties or school dances.

The emotional and physical scars have affected her confidence as an adult.

"I wear lots of makeup and practically live in my sunglasses," she said, tears welling up in her eyes. "I even grocery shop late at night to avoid conversation with people I know."

"I'm sorry," was all I could say as I handed her a tissue.

"It's so silly and petty," she said. She rolled her eyes and shook her head. "I hate making a big deal about it, but the fear in my heart and mind is crippling at times."

"It's not silly and it's not petty," I assured her. "It's real."

God says, "Do not be afraid," 366 times in the Bible. That's one challenge for every day of the year including leap year. But it's easier said than done.

When the big, scary, emotional monster of insecurity is chasing us toward isolation and seclusion, how do we keep from cowering in fear? When the warmth of Satan's breath can be felt on the backs of our necks, when he's lying to us about who we really are, how do we stand our ground? How do we take ground from the enemy of our souls?

We look at Jesus.

The Bible says that Jesus was tempted in every possible way. Satan tried to scare Jesus. For forty days he threatened Jesus, he lied to Jesus, he accused Jesus. Satan treated Jesus the same way he treats us.

Satan is a cosmic bully who wants to take more than our lunch money from us. He wants to beat the life out of us that God has put in us.

When I was in college, some friends of mine went to a fire tower in the woods late at night to hang out. The towers were used years ago to scout out forest fires, so they rise about fifty feet above the treetops. And the one my friends went to had been abandoned decades before.

I didn't go with them, but I went.

A few hours after they left campus, I put on dark clothing and made my way to the clearing in the woods near the fire tower. I could hear them, but I couldn't see them. It was an overcast night, with clouds blocking the normal glow of the moon. I couldn't see my hand in front of my face. It was a perfect night to scare some friends.

I crawled within fifty feet of the picnic table where they were sitting and even stood up without them realizing I was there.

Have you ever wanted to scare someone, and in the process of scaring them, you got scared? As I was standing there in total darkness, I got the impression that I wasn't alone. I got the impression that someone was standing right in front of me.

I stopped breathing.

And that's when I heard it. I heard the voice of a friend say, "Hey guys, I think someone is standing right in front of me."

It was one of my best friends who happened to be into bodybuilding. His arms were bigger and more muscular than my legs. He was cut and chiseled and twice the man that I was. But he sounded scared. His voice cracked and quivered, and the next time he spoke, he sounded panicked.

"Someone is standing right in front of me," he said to the group.

I wanted to laugh, but I was too afraid that he would deck me. So I closed my eyes and braced for the blow.

"Quit joking around," someone yelled from the picnic table.

"I'm not joking. Someone is out here," he fired back.

I couldn't have asked for a better scenario. So with all my might, I lowered my voice and yelled, "You punks better get off my land!"

In that moment, every bladder of every person at that picnic table emptied as all of them screamed and scattered.

It was total chaos, and it was beautiful.

I chased after my friend Amber, primarily because she was the slowest runner in the group, but also because she was the most paranoid. As I chased her through the woods, I would reach out my hand every so often, touch the back of her head, and say, "You're mine!" I had never heard Amber cuss until that night. She made sailors seem like choirboys.

Everyone jumped into cars, and tires screeched as they peeled off.

The next morning at breakfast, everyone at the table was reliving the night of horror from their vantage point. And that's when my buddy—who could've been the poster boy for steroids—said, "We could have died out there!"

I thought I was going to choke on my Cheerios! Milk sprayed out my nose, and I had to dismiss myself from the table. Had they known I was the source of their fear, they wouldn't have been afraid. When I flex my muscles, my son says, "Are you flexing yet?"

Satan wants us to believe that he's stronger and scarier than he really is.

I don't want to underestimate his abilities because he is cunning. But he's also predictable. He knows our weakest areas because our weakest areas are on display for the world to see. And that's what he exploits.

Some people are afraid to die. We don't know when we're going to die or how we're going to die, which creates fear in a lot of people. Satan loves to convince people who are afraid of dying that they need to go to the doctor every week or buy more life insurance. He keeps them from living for fear of dying.

For others, it's a fear of rejection, so they live to please everyone around them. But you can't make everybody happy, and no one will approve of everything you do.

Author Jesse Rice posted this letter online, addressing his fear of what others think about him:

> Dear Fear-Of-What-Others-Think:
>
> I am sick of you, and it's time we broke up. I know we've broken up and gotten back together many times, but seriously, Fear-Of-What-Others-Think, *this is it*. We're breaking up.
>
> I'm tired of over-thinking my status updates on Facebook, trying to sound more clever, funny, and important. I'm sick of feeling anxious about what I say or do in public, especially around people I don't know that well, all in the hope that they'll like me, accept me, praise me. I run around all day feeling like a Golden Retriever with a full bladder: Like me! Like me! Like me!
>
> Because of you, I go through my day with a cloud of shame hanging over my head, and I never stop acting. The spotlight's always on, and I'm center stage, and I'd better keep dancing, posturing, mugging, or else the spotlight will move, and I'll dissolve

into a little, meaningless puddle on the ground, just like that witch in *The Wizard of Oz*. I can never live up to the expectations of my imaginary audience, the one that lives only in my head but whose collective voice is louder than any other voice in the universe.

And all of this is especially evil because if I really stop and think about it, and let things go quiet and listen patiently for the voice of the God who made me and the Savior who died for me, in his eyes, it turns out I'm actually—profoundly—precious, lovable, worthy, valuable, and even just a little ghetto-fabulous. When I find my true identity in Christ, then you turn back into the tiny, yapping little dog that you are.

So eat it, Fear-Of-What-Others-Think. You and I are done. And no, I'm not interested in "talking it through." I'm running, jumping, laughing you out of my life, once and for all. Or at least, that's what I really, really want . . . God help me!"[1]

When I walk out to preach each weekend, there is always a lump in my throat. Standing up in front of large crowds of people has never come easily or naturally to me. What I've learned in the middle of those knee-knocking moments is that God doesn't give us courage when we're afraid. Instead, he reminds us of his presence and his power and his promise to never leave us.

"You're not on this stage alone," is what he whispers to me each weekend.

God gives us circumstances where we either take a step toward our fear or run in retreat. If you face your fear, that's when courage floods into your heart. That's when you see God smiling and cheering you on.

It's also when you see Satan.

Once you see Satan for who he really is and what he really wants to do, you realize how important it is to face your fear. Facing a fear requires faith. And faith pleases God. When you put your faith in him, you are saying, "God, I believe your power is greater than my fear." That makes God's heart race!

When your fear is replaced with faith, that's when you experience this incredible gift called freedom. God wants to exchange the fear in your heart for freedom.

So, the question isn't, "What are you afraid of?" The question is, "Where is your faith?"

Are you trusting in your own ability or in God's?

4

PERSONALITY: BAYWATCH, BEETHOVEN, AND BACON

SEVERAL YEARS AGO THE STAFF AT OUR CHURCH SCHEDULED A RETREAT at a lodge deep in the woods. The goal of the retreat was to build team unity, so we engaged in several team-building activities. One evening we set chairs up in a circle so each person could see everyone else on the team. Our executive pastor kicked the activity off by asking a question.

"If you could spend the day with one person, who would it be and why?"

As I thought about the person I would most want to spend a day with, it was fun to hear the other staff members' answers. A lot of people talked about loved ones who had died that they missed. Some people talked about characters from the Bible like Noah and David and Jesus. Other people mentioned their spouse or a best friend.

We laughed, we cried, and after a hundred people shared, the last person in the circle was our custodian, Jimmy. He is one of my favorite people on the planet. He's worked at our church for a long time and is like a little brother to all of us. We love him and look out for him.

He held the microphone up to his mouth, and I think all of us thought he would mention his brother who had died recently or his parents who passed away when he was younger. No one was ready for what came out of his mouth.

"If I could spend the day with anyone," he said in a very sincere voice, "I would like to spend it with Pamela Anderson or Drew Barrymore."

Forget Shadrach, Meshach, and Abednego. He had *Baywatch* and *Charlie's Angels* on his mind!

I've never seen our staff laugh so hard, and I've never seen Jimmy smile so big.

I've always been a discerning person. Often I can tell when something is bothering someone. But even with a knack for appraising a situation, I've come to realize that I don't always know what is going on in other people's heads and hearts. Most days, I'm a pretty simple and fairly predictable guy. My wife, my kids, and the people I work with would tell you I'm easy to read.

But I have my moments when I'm not really sure what I'm feeling and why I'm feeling the way I do. There are parts of my head and my heart that are yet to be explored and mapped.

Can you imagine how incredible it must have been to be Columbus—to be the very first person from the Old World to see the New World? Can you imagine what it was like when his boat hit the island of Hispaniola, and as far as the eye could see, there were white sand beaches and lush rain forests?

Or can you imagine the moment when Scottish explorer David Livingstone was cutting his way through the jungles of Africa and he stumbled across Victoria Falls? Whatever hardships and sickness and difficulty he endured to traverse the continent of Africa was probably worth it in that moment, when the massive waterfall came into view.

Or can you imagine what it must have felt like for Neil Armstrong to be the very first human being ever to step foot on the moon? You know his adrenaline was pumping in that moment!

I'm convinced the greatest unexplored frontier in the universe is your life, because no two lives are the same. And yet isn't it fascinating that many of us look alike, dress alike, talk alike, think alike, and act alike?

Every culture has a mold (a cookie cutter), but I would love for you to be as adventurous as Lewis and Clark and get inside your heart to explore what's really in there. Because when God made you, he broke the mold. You are the one and only you. There will never be another you. Never! What all of us have in common is that we were all created in God's image. And think about how vast God is. Think about how big God is. Think about how there is no end to God.

God wants you to discover his larger-than-life image in you.

At my daughter's piano recital I heard the same song played in different ways by different kids at different skill levels. The younger kids looked at the keys and played slowly and deliberately. I knew the tune, but it wasn't until the older kids played the song that it started to sound like what Beethoven probably had in mind when he composed it.

We have to look to Jesus to know what God had in mind when he created us. Many of us live our lives the way a first-year piano student plays Beethoven—cautiously and predictably. But when I see a concert pianist play, the music flows through them in the same way that God wants his life to flow through us.

In the New Testament, Saul had become what everyone else around him thought he should become. He was a Pharisee because his teacher was a Pharisee. Saul allowed his life to be defined by the mold, by the cookie cutter. And when Jesus died, rose, and ascended to heaven, the movement of Christ's followers exploded with growth. Saul did everything he could to stop them, even going so far as murdering them. He did what everyone expected him to do. He played it safe.

Ever had a friend who votes Democrat because someone in

their family was a Democrat or they vote Republican because someone in their family was a Republican? Or ever had a friend who was a Catholic or a Baptist because someone in their family was a Catholic or a Baptist? Or have you ever had a friend who was a teacher or a lawyer because someone in their family was a teacher or a lawyer?

It's the cookie cutter. It's playing "Ode to Joy" with two fingers instead of two hands.

Saul understood the pressure to settle and to conform. Jesus met Saul on a road and freed him from that pressure. He even changed Saul's name to Paul so he could have a fresh start. And that fresh start is a common theme in Paul's writing.

If I could sum my point up in a sentence, I'd say: your past is not your past if it still impacts your present. When God looks at you, he doesn't say, "Oh, there's so-and-so's daughter. Oh, there's so-and-so's brother or sister. Oh, there's so-and-so's best friend."

No, when God looks at you, he sees you.

At some point in every person's life they have to evaluate the good and the bad of their past experiences. They must decide that they want to move forward, to be the person that God made them to be and not the person that everyone expects or wants them to be. And that's not easy!

Saul stayed in Damascus for three days, blind and without food. Sometimes I wonder if it wouldn't help us if we could close our eyes for an extended period of time and replay the tape of our lives to see just how much our past affects our present.

I did that this week. After sitting still and thinking with my eyes closed for thirty minutes, I ended up taking a friend to lunch and apologizing to him. I had been frustrated with him for the behavior of one of his friends. Instead of taking it out on his friend, I took it out on him! And it had hurt our friendship, so I owned it— because I don't want last year to affect next year.

While getting dressed recently, I missed a button on my shirt, and by the time I got to the top button, my entire shirt was out of whack. The fabric pulled against itself and nothing lined up or looked right. There were gaping holes exposing parts of me that I wanted to cover up.

Many of us feel as though something in our lives is missing, and we wish it were as easy to see as a button on a shirt. Perhaps something in our upbringing was missing, and by the time we're adults, it's tough to pinpoint why we feel out of sorts. All we know is something is out of alignment, and one part of our being is tugging against another and exposing parts we want to cover up.

Years ago I received a letter from a woman whose dad was addicted to alcohol and pornography when she was a kid. His addictions damaged her family, and in the letter she reflected upon how it made her feel.

"I feel like my dad was a red shirt in a white load of laundry, tainting everybody else with his actions."

She had to decide not to let his past affect her future.

My sister Julie volunteers in an elementary school. She tutors at-risk children, and there is a little boy named Christopher who has captured her attention and affection. Christopher's' mom dropped him off for the first day of kindergarten and never came back to get him. He hasn't seen his mom since.

So every day when Christopher walks to the cafeteria for lunch, the school's principal invites him into his office and the two of them call Christopher's dad. And every day Christopher asks his dad the same question: "Dad, are you going to pick me up today?"

He's afraid, and rightfully so, because the person who was supposed to run to Christopher ran from him.

I'm a lot like that little boy. I need reassurance from my Father that he's going to show up and pick me up in this crazy world. I need God to remind me that he won't abandon me to a world filled with school shootings and terrorist attacks.

If you don't let God transform your past, you will transfer it into your future. Let him transform your hurt into hope and your fear into faith. You don't want to be weighed down by someone else's baggage.

When your desire to heal is greater than your desire to hide, you will heal.

I have a friend who was a male prostitute and sold himself to other men for sex. He's now an incredible husband and dad. And it all started when he quit hiding and let God heal him.

After Adam and Eve sinned, they hid from God. But God came looking for them. Genesis says, "At that moment their eyes were opened" (3:7 NLT). Like you, like me, like Saul, like my friend who sold himself, Adam and Eve realized their need for God and finally saw themselves the way that God saw them.

The scales fell from their eyes.

I baptized a college-aged Muslim named Sarah. Several friends of hers are Christians, and the loving way they treated her created a curiosity in her about their faith.

In an e-mail to me, she wrote,

> I was born a Muslim and my whole family is Muslim. But God gave me the opportunity to explore Christianity by having me come to the United States and by putting certain people in my life. As a Muslim you have to earn your way to heaven by your works, and as we all know that is very difficult to do since we are all sinners. I constantly felt like I needed to do more and I felt like my relationship with the Muslim god had to be earned. But with Christianity I felt loved from the very beginning even before I converted. I felt a relationship with Jesus that is unexplainable. It hit me a few weeks ago that I have

the option to believe in a God who loves me with all of my flaws. A God who gave his only Son to die for all of my mistakes, which are plenty! All I know is that I have never been more at peace, more joyous, and all I want to do is lead people to him.

I once was blind, but now I see.

After I baptized her, the first thing she said was, "Now I can eat bacon!" Muslims don't eat pork, so she was most excited about this. Not forgiveness of sins, not living in heaven forever . . . bacon!

If you love bacon, Jesus loves you!

I was recently introduced to a man named David who lives in Jerusalem. He converted from Islam to Christianity years ago and has been beaten and threatened multiple times for sharing his faith. The last time it happened, he smuggled eight hundred Bibles into the Dome of the Rock, a mosque that sits on the Temple Mount in Jerusalem. When he started passing them out to young Muslim men, some older Muslim men grabbed him, held a knife to his throat, and told him they were going to cut his head off if he didn't stop. He laughed at them.

"If you cut off my head," he told them, "it will roll down the hill singing, 'Thank you, Jesus! Thank you, Jesus!'"

Who could say such a thing? Someone who has discovered who God made them to be.

Be you. Not the version the world wants you to be, but the person God created you to be.

5

IDENTITY: YOU, ME, AND E.T.

WHEN WE MOVED OUT OF OUR HOUSE, I MADE ONE FINAL TRIP TO gather up the belongings we had failed to pack. I was tired and hot and ready to be done, so I threw all of the remaining books and shoes and toys in one giant box. I didn't realize how heavy the box was until I squatted down to pick it up. And it was heavy.

I didn't want to bother anyone, so I grunted and groaned and manhandled the box. As I made my way to the staircase, I realized I couldn't see the first step around the box. Instead of setting the box down and sliding it down the stairs, I did what most men in my shoes would do—I went for it.

I would like to say I tripped on the first step, but I didn't even hit the first step. And I really can't even say that I fell, because I flew—from the top step to the bottom step.

I hit the wall at the bottom of the steps so violently that the entire house shook. I was convinced that internal bleeding had begun. But when you fall like that, the last thing you're worried about is your physical well-being. The first thing you're worried about is if someone saw you fall!

Once I realized no one had seen me, I gathered up my dignity and the stuff that had fallen out of the box and walked to our truck. As I set the box down on the tailgate, a little girl rode up on her scooter and said, "Mr. Weece, what was that noise?"

"What noise?" I asked, a surprised look on my face.

"It sounded like something exploded in your house," she said as she pointed toward my house.

"It's not polite to be nosy!" I said. "Beat it!"

Actually, I didn't say that, but I wanted to.

All of us carry around things that weigh us down, knock us down, and keep us from becoming the people God created us to be.

I love looking at the covers of magazines as I'm standing in line at the grocery store. Publishers make promises they can't keep: "Buy this product, do this exercise, wear this outfit, and your life will be so much better."

As a result of these empty promises, many of us keep scales in our bathrooms, and when we don't weigh what our culture tells us we should weigh, we get discouraged.

I've decided to create a bathroom scale that talks to you when you stand on it. Instead of rattling off your weight, it's going to say things such as, "You only live once. Eat more Oreos!"

If you haven't eaten Golden Oreos, you are sinning.

We live in a performance-based culture. For many in our culture there is the unspoken mantra: "What you do defines who you are." We're fed a lie. We're told our identities are determined by either our failures or successes. On one end of the spectrum are people with a deflated view of themselves, who say things such as, "I failed in school. I failed in business. I failed in marriage. Therefore, I am a failure."

That is a lie.

On the other end of the spectrum are people with an inflated view of themselves. They say things such as, "I am stronger, prettier, wealthier, and smarter than you. Therefore, I am better than you."

That is also a lie.

What you do does not define who you are. You can fail academically and athletically and still be a successful person. More importantly, you can be a loved person. Your identity is not achieved; your identity is received.

Calvin Miller once wrote, "For most who live, hell is never knowing who they are."[1]

Sadly, that is true for so many people. They do not know that God defines us and bases our identity on the performance of his Son. Jesus' work on the cross and in the tomb determines our value. Obviously God thinks a lot about us.

What we do does not define who we are.

What does define us? God's intense love for us. God calls us sons and daughters. And he adds words like *cherished* and *chosen* to emphasize just how much he loves us.

God doesn't see us the way we see ourselves.

After years of wrestling with my identity and watching others wrestle with theirs, I learned this important truth: bad assumptions lead to bad assessments. Some people assume they're worse than they really are, while other people assume they're better than they really are.

"Be honest in your evaluation of yourselves," Paul wrote in Romans 12:3 (NLT). Honesty is a key that unlocks our identity.

One afternoon, a man pulled into the parking lot of our church, rolled his windows down, turned off the engine, and just sat in the front seat for hours. My antennae are always up for people who isolate themselves, so after an hour of watching him through my office window, I finally went out to check on him.

"Hey, I'm Jon. I saw you sitting out here and wondered if I could do anything for you," I said.

"I lost my job eighteen months ago. I've burned through all of my savings. My wife and kids are frustrated with me, and I'm frustrated with myself," he said as the tears began to flow. "I don't feel like a man. Men are supposed to provide for their families, and I can't provide for mine."

Satan was whispering lies to him. Satan wants us to believe that what we do defines who we are.

I invited him to hang out with me in my office, and I called a fun friend of mine who has a lot of time and a lot of money. Bob showed up and listened to the man's story. Then Bob pulled out his checkbook and wrote the guy a check.

"I'm not trying to buy your friendship," Bob said as he slid the check across the table. "I just want to alleviate some of the pressure you are carrying around right now."

"I can't accept this," the guy said as he shook his head in disbelief. "This is twice the amount that I need."

"Let me explain something to you," Bob said, a huge smile on his face. "God gives me more forgiveness than I deserve so I can give you more money than you deserve."

We have a different leader, so we live by a different law. We speak a different language. Peter referred to us as "aliens." I remember reading that as a kid and thinking, "I love E.T., but I don't think I look a thing like him." I do wish my finger could light up like his. Think about how handy that would be.

If you ever feel as though you don't belong, it's because you don't. If you ever feel as though something's missing, it's because it is. We are aliens. This is not our home.

P. T. Forsyth once wrote, "If within us we find nothing above us, we succumb to what is around us."[2]

I hear people say all the time, "I don't feel like myself," or, "That is not something I would normally do." Amid those "out-of-body" experiences when we say and do things we later regret, we're trying to reconcile what is above us with what is going on around us. Psychology refers to this as "languishing." You'll hear people speak of a dead-end job or a dead marriage. They're alive, but they feel as if they're surrounded by death on all sides.

And they are.

What is above us is life. But what is around us is death.

God is life—the author of it, the sustainer of it, the giver of it. And we were created in his image. God is the Creator. God made something out of nothing, which makes God an artist. And if we were created in his image, what does that make us?

We too are artists—hardwired by God to add strokes of beauty to the world around us. When we fail to do that, we languish. We die.

ME TOO

All of us were meant to add a verse to the song, a color to the canvas, and a scene to the script of the grand story that is unfolding around us.

The Fifth Symphony was in Beethoven. It just had to be drawn out of him.

The *Mona Lisa* was in da Vinci. It just had to be drawn out of him.

The secret recipe was in Colonel Sanders! And I'm so glad he didn't keep it a secret.

What piece of the God-puzzle is in you that the world needs to see, so then they can see God better? The older we get, the less we believe we have something to offer. The older we get, the more we die and the less we live.

My son woke up with a stomachache a few weeks ago. He rolled around on the couch in pain and said, "I think this is what it feels like to get shot!"

He said it in a very heroic way, as if he had been mortally wounded while storming the beaches of Normandy. As the night went on, the pain got worse and worse, so we finally took him to the emergency room at a local hospital. We thought he might have appendicitis.

On the exam table in the ER, he looked at his mom and said, "Mom, if I don't make it out of here alive . . . I just want you to know that I love you." He really thought he was going to die!

It turns out his appendix was fine, but he had eaten an inhuman amount of chips and salsa the night before.

G. K. Chesterton once observed:

> Because children have abounding vitality, because they are in spirit fierce and free, therefore they want things repeated and unchanged. They always say, "Do it again"; and the grown-up person does it again until he is nearly dead. For grown-up people are not strong enough to live in monotony. But perhaps God is strong enough to exult in monotony. It is possible that God says every morning, "Do it again" to the sun; and every evening, "Do it again" to the moon. It may not be automatic necessity that makes all daisies alike; it may be that God makes every daisy separately, but has never got tired of making them. It may be that He has the eternal appetite of infancy; for we have sinned and grown old, and our Father is younger than we.[3]

Could it be that everything God touches gets better with time? Including you?

Over time, every living thing on earth ages and eventually dies. When I cut into a watermelon, I'm forced to eat it within a few days. But what if each bite tasted better than the previous bite? What if ice cream never melted? What if your energy increased, your mental capacity expanded, and your ability to experience joy grew over time?

What if you became the person God created you to be?

ME TOO

My daughter loves to watch old home videos. For hours on end she will watch old clips of birthday parties and vacations at the beach and Christmas mornings. It puts the biggest smile on her face because as a seventh grader, she doesn't find life as easy as it once was. The world has a way of robbing us of our innocence. It conditions us to die when we were created to live.

I recently attended the wedding of some friends who rearranged the traditional ceremony. When guests arrived, they were ushered into a big tent where there was food and music and games. Everyone was having a good time! Meanwhile, in a nearby field and under a beautiful willow tree, our friends were getting married. Surrounded by close family, all we could do was watch at a distance.

But when they arrived, I had the privilege of introducing them to the crowd as a married couple for the first time. Everyone went crazy! The noise shot up several decibels as people hooted and hollered and welcomed the newlyweds to their own party.

I think heaven is going to be a lot like that. The book of Revelation describes heaven as "a bride beautifully dressed for her husband" (21:2 NLT).

A party started two thousand years ago when Jesus defeated death, and when you show up, everyone will go crazy! It will feel like everyone was waiting on you to walk in because you make the party better.

And you'll finally feel comfortable in your own skin. You will be you. The real you. You won't be measured by failures or successes. You'll be known as the son or daughter that you are. His son or his daughter.

Until that day and even today, don't let anyone tell you that you can't be a kid again.

HUMILITY: *KINTSUGI*

I RECENTLY HAD MY PARATHYROID GLAND, MY APPENDIX, AND MY gallbladder removed.

I returned from a trip to Haiti with typhoid and spent a few days in the hospital. During that stay, doctors discovered a few abnormalities in my blood work.

I had felt bad for a few years but pushed through the physical and emotional discomfort thinking it would eventually subside. But it never did. The typhoid gave me the excuse I needed to get checked out.

As they wheeled me into the operating room, a sweet nurse walked beside me. Once I was settled onto the bed they would use to perform the surgery, the anesthesiologist gave me a shot to relax me and help me fall asleep.

As I drifted into the deepest sleep of my life, the nurse pulled her mask down, smiled at me, and said, "I go to the church where you preach and I love it!"

I smiled and mumbled something I don't remember. But I do remember what she said next: "I'm going to remove your gown and shave you."

Up to that point in my life, my mom and my wife and a few buddies in college were the only people who had ever seen me naked. But now a nurse who sits in the audience I preach to every week has seen me in all my glory!

I am so grateful for HIPAA laws and patient confidentiality agreements.

Over the years I've learned that humiliation can lead to humility. And humility isn't thinking less of yourself. Humility is thinking of yourself less.

According to Greek mythology there was a young man named Narcissus who was so good-looking that he couldn't take his eyes off himself. As the story goes, when he looked into a pool of water and saw his reflection, he was so enamored with it he just sat and stared for hours. Hours turned to days, and Narcissus stared so long he starved to death.

He died because he refused to take his eyes off himself.

All of us have blind spots. All of us have weaknesses and

challenges and issues that keep us from being the people God created us to be. Maybe you dominate conversations and you don't know it. Maybe you violate people's personal space or you want to appear smarter than you are. Maybe you name-drop so you seem more popular than you are. The truth about you and me is that we don't always know the truth about ourselves, and we need other people to tell us what they see.

Other than Jesus, the person who is mentioned the most in the Bible is a guy named David. I think it's because we're all like David and he's like all of us. David had several blind spots. At one point in his life his power went to his head and he slept with a woman who wasn't his wife. He thought he could get away with it by having her husband killed, which he also thought he could get away with. One dumb action led to several dumb actions.

When one of David's friends, a man named Nathan, learned what David had done, he confronted him in a subtle way. He told David a story to help him see what he couldn't see on his own— something that everyone else around him could see. Nathan said,

> There were two men in a certain town. One was rich, and one was poor. The rich man owned a great many sheep and cattle. The poor man owned nothing but one little lamb he had bought. He raised that little lamb, and it grew up with his children. It ate from the man's own plate and drank from his cup. He cuddled it in his arms like a baby daughter. One day a guest arrived at the home of the rich man. But instead of killing an animal from his

own flock or herd, he took the poor man's lamb and killed it and prepared it for his guest." David was furious. "As surely as the Lord lives," he vowed, "any man who would do such a thing deserves to die! He must repay four lambs to the poor man for the one he stole and for having no pity." Then Nathan said to David, "You are that man!" (2 Sam. 12:1–7 NLT)

The opposite of self-awareness is self-deception. And if the truth can set us free, a lie can hold us hostage.

Pete Wilson is a good friend and the pastor of a church in Nashville. He wrote a prayer that I've used to create a pathway for greater awareness: "Father, let me know as much truth about me as I can handle."[1]

One roadblock to us seeing what God sees is the pace of our lives. Satan wants us to move through life so fast so that we don't slow down and see the toxic stuff that poisons our hearts.

We live in a culture that foolishly wears busyness as a badge of honor. It's not only dumb; it's damaging every aspect of our lives. So we have to learn to embrace the spiritual gift of slowness, which seems impossible in a culture that believes faster is better.

We have an old couch in our playroom—an L-shaped sectional that we bought when we were first married. Recently we had a house full of kids spending the night, so I went to the playroom to fix places for the kids to sleep. I hadn't been in there since the last sleepover.

When I took the cushions off the couch, I found M&M's, popcorn, Nerf bullets, Legos, and one dirty, wadded-up sock. "I want a raise! I am not getting paid enough for the work I do!" I said as I carried the sock to the trash can.

I bet God looks at what's in my heart, the stuff I try to keep hidden, the stuff I try not to think about—the debris, the crumbs, the dirty stuff from decisions I made years ago—and he wishes he could remove that weight so I could have a good night's rest.

I have a few routines in my day that allow me to pull back the cushions and look beyond what everyone else sees in my life. One of them is walking to a pond near our house after work. I don't own the pond, but I've stocked it with bass, bluegill, and catfish, and I feed the fish growing in the pond because someday I want to catch them. But the main reason I walk to the pond every evening is to deal with my blind spots.

I've learned that awareness increases as hurry decreases.

In his book *The Life You've Always Wanted*, author John Ortberg offers this wise observation about the pace of our lives: "The truth is, as much as we complain about it, we are drawn to hurry. It makes us feel important. It keeps the adrenaline pumping. It means we don't have to look too closely at the heart or life. It keeps us from feeling our loneliness."[2]

A few weeks ago I flew into Chicago at night. As we approached the city at four hundred miles per hour, the skyline looked cool, but I couldn't see all of it because of how fast we were going. Then I got in my rental car and drove past the city at seventy-five miles per hour, and it was cool to see the city from a car; but again, I couldn't focus on anything because of the speed. When I got out of the car and walked onto the campus of Moody Bible Institute in downtown Chicago, my entire perspective changed because I was walking at two miles per hour.

The trees, the architecture, the height of the buildings, the people, the smell of the ethnic food being cooked: all of it took on a different feel because of the speed at which I was moving.

We drive and put on our makeup while eating an Egg McMuffin and drinking our Starbucks and checking our e-mail, and we don't call it a sickness. We call it multitasking. So many of us are hurrying through life at four hundred miles per hour, and we can't enjoy our relationships or our jobs or anything else for that matter because it's just too fast, too hectic.

Psalm 46:10 says, "Be *still,* and know that I am God" (NIV, emphasis mine). Hurrying through life means we don't trust God to take care of us. Slowing down communicates a high level of trust in him. So schedule time in your day to slow down and enjoy your relationships with people and with God.

I call it "intentional inactivity."

Our culture is terrified of silence, but God created us to work and withdraw. Jesus modeled that rhythm. If I don't honor that pace, I crash and burn. When I don't slow down, I wear down.

But as I slow down, I begin to see what I haven't been able to see before—such as my perfectionistic tendencies, which put unrealistic pressure on me and everyone around me. Maybe if you would slow down, you would see why you procrastinate, why you're always buried under a pile of clutter, or why you're so competitive at things that don't matter, or why you're nice to strangers and mean to the people you love.

Some friends of mine have a son with Down syndrome. The dad is a football coach, and for years they lived in Texas. During their fifteen years in Dallas, their son thrived in the church they attended. Everyone in the church knew and loved Mark, and there wasn't a Sunday when he didn't help collect the offering and pass out the Communion. He was a fixture in the church family, and Sunday was Mark's favorite day of the week.

But his dad was fired from his coaching position and had to take a new job in St. Louis. As the family adjusted to life in a new city, they finally found a church to call home. But Mark didn't like it. Every Sunday he would ask his parents if he could stay home. His parents knew it would take time for Mark to get to know the people of the church and for the people of the church to get to know Mark. So every Sunday, Mark's parents insisted he go to church with them.

One Sunday morning, a man in the church approached Mark and said, "Someone left a gift for you in the lobby."

Mark stood up, raced down the center aisle, and ran out of the sanctuary and into the lobby. On the counter at the welcome center was a huge jar of M&M's. M&M's were Mark's favorite candy!

Attached to the jar was a note that read, "We're glad you're a part of our church family!" That gift changed everything.

Every Sunday, Mark looked forward to going to church, and every Sunday until Mark's death at forty-six years of age, an anonymous person left a jar of M&M's at the welcome center in the lobby for him.

Someone wise once told me that the church moves at the pace of its slowest member. When we slow down, we not only begin to see what's broken in our lives, but we also begin to see what's broken in the people around us. The church was meant to be a safe place for everyone, everywhere, to heal together—a surgery center where the Great Physician puts us back together again.

Author William MacDonald wrote, "Usually when something is broken, its value declines or disappears altogether. Broken dishes, broken bottles, broken mirrors are generally scrapped. Even a crack in furniture or a tear in cloth greatly reduces its resale value. But it isn't that way in the spiritual realm. God puts a premium on broken things—especially broken people."[3]

Once we become aware of our brokenness and acknowledge it, that's when God is able to do what only he can: repair the damaged areas of our lives.

In the Old Testament, God had a conversation with a prophet named Jeremiah. God said, "Go down to the potter's house, and there I will give you my message." So Jeremiah went down to the potter's house and noted what he observed:

I saw him working at the wheel. But the pot he was shaping from the clay was marred in his hands; so the potter formed it into another pot, shaping it as seemed best to him.

Then the word of the LORD came to me. He said, "Can I not do with you, Israel, as this potter does?" declares the LORD. "Like clay in the hand of the potter, so are you in my hand, Israel." (Jer. 18:1–6 NIV)

There is an interesting ancient ceramic restoration technique called *Kintsugi* that is popular in Japan. Instead of hiding the cracks in a piece of pottery, the repair accentuates them; it highlights them with a beautiful adhesive that includes gold or silver. Some of the most expensive pieces of pottery in Japanese history were once broken, but were delicately and intricately put back together again.

God wants to do the same thing with you. He wants to take the part of your life that you want to hide—that you don't want others to see—and he wants to highlight it so the world can see what he's capable of doing.

Brokenness for beauty. Humiliation for humility.

Slow down so the rest of us can help you. Slow down so God can heal you.

7

RECEPTIVITY: SOME DIRT UNDER THEIR NAILS

MY FIRST GRADE TEACHER, MRS. SMITH, WAS SO SWEET AND BEAUTIFUL, and she had a southern accent that I could listen to for hours. As a matter of fact, I used to raise my hand and ask for help even when I didn't need help because I loved hearing her talk. And she smelled good too. I can remember thinking, *Mrs. Smith uses a different soap than me!*

While most of my friends were in love with Farrah Fawcett, I was smitten with Mrs. Smith.

On the totally opposite end of the spectrum was my sixth-grade teacher, Mrs. Wacker. She was as mean as her name sounds—WACKER!

Behind her back we called her Eva Braun, which was the name of Hitler's girlfriend. Eva Braun died in a bunker in Berlin, but she had been reincarnated as a sixth-grade teacher in Missouri.

One of my favorite teachers was a high school history teacher named Mr. Taylor. I don't know if it was the subject matter or the way he taught, but he pushed me and challenged me to think for myself. He created an environment in his classroom where it was safe to ask questions, debate, and share opinions. I loved being a student in his class.

I also had a college professor who took me under his wing and invited me into his life. I graded papers for him, drove him to speaking engagements, did research with him, and more importantly, watched how he treated his wife and kids. I still call him when I have questions about the Bible.

There are few things worse in life than a bad teacher, and few things better in life than a great teacher.

Jesus was a teacher, and his students were called disciples. Twelve young men spent the better part of three years learning from him.

Jesus often taught by telling stories called parables. A parable is an earthly story with a heavenly meaning. It was Jesus' creative way of engaging his audience and keeping their attention while delivering a compelling lesson about life.

One day Jesus told a story about a farmer who scattered some seed on the ground. Some of the seed fell on good soil, while the rest of the seed fell on soil that was threatened by weeds and thorns and rocks and birds.

The seed that fell on good soil thrived. The seed that fell on bad soil died.

The seed represents life and all the good stuff God wants to develop in the hearts of people: love, joy, peace, patience, kindness, goodness, faithfulness, and self-control. The Bible calls it fruit.

Your heart will either receive or reject the life that Jesus wants to grow in you, and it all comes down to the roots. If the roots are good, the plant will be good. If the roots are bad, the plant will be bad. Good roots lead to good results.

When I was a kid, we had a garden in our backyard, and my siblings and I worked in it with our dad. He would say things such as, "Jon, you can't plant a pumpkin seed and expect a watermelon to grow. Pumpkin seeds create pumpkins. Watermelon seeds create watermelons."

That seemed so obvious to me as a kid, but it was what my dad said next that I've never forgotten. "Jon, good friends lead to a good life. Bad friends lead to a bad life," he said with concern. "Water the good relationships and weed out the bad."

The Bible explains it this way: "You will always harvest what you plant" (Gal. 6:7 NLT). Whatever influence you allow to be planted in your heart is what will grow in your life.

ME TOO

Many people we love and care about have had nothing but bad seeds planted in the soil of their lives, and the outcome has been predictable. They've never experienced a spiritual harvest of goodness and love—only drought and famine and hunger for something better than what they've tasted. The fruit of this life can be sour, leaving a bad aftertaste in the mouths of many.

Jesus taught that second chances are possible. A person doesn't have to be who they've always been. In the same way that one bad crop doesn't define the farmer, one bad season in a person's life doesn't define that person. Dead plants can always be uprooted and replaced with better seed.

"Me too" people gladly share their farming secrets with those who are struggling to grow. And the greatest farming secret we have tucked away in the pockets of our overalls is Jesus: the Vine, the Holy Spirit, the Gardener. We're just a bunch of branches that he wants to hang his fruit on. And when we surrender to his pruning, we experience the growth we've always longed to see.

Give the Holy Spirit permission to uproot what needs to be uprooted in your life. I'm learning that his work in my heart isn't always pleasant, but it is productive, and it's most productive when I take good care of the soil in my heart. Most of the spiritual erosion I've experienced in my life is due to what I've allowed to creep into the garden of my heart.

Growing up, my family had a television that only got two

channels: NBC and CBS. If we wanted to watch ABC, we had to move the antenna around. After I got a cavity filled in one of my back teeth, my older brothers convinced me that I would be a better transmitter of the signal, so I would stand for long periods of time holding the antenna with one hand and my mouth wide open. They swore we got a better picture when I did that.

My favorite shows growing up were *The Dukes of Hazzard* and *Diff'rent Strokes*, and my mom let me invite my neighborhood buddies over to watch them with me. But when my neighborhood buddies invited me to watch television at their houses, I wasn't allowed to go. Everyone was allowed to come in our house, but I wasn't allowed to go into anyone else's house.

What determined if I was allowed to go to a friend's house was whether or not they had this new piece of technology called cable television. I wasn't allowed to watch MTV and HBO, and though I didn't totally understand why, I trusted my mom because I knew that she loved me. As an adult, I now know even more why she wanted me to guard my heart.

Billy Graham asked every hotel he ever stayed in to remove the TV before he arrived so he wouldn't be tempted to watch things he shouldn't watch while he was away from his wife and children. I have a buddy who is in sales, so he travels a lot. He keeps a picture of his wife and kids on the dashboard of his car so he's not tempted to pull off at one of those pornography stores alongside the interstate.

"If I wouldn't feel comfortable walking in with my daughters," he reminds himself, "it's not a place I should go."

My friend Phil keeps a piece of cardboard wrapped around his remote control at home. Every time he goes to turn on the television, he has to remove the cardboard, and that simple act reminds him that he doesn't want to be entertained by the sin Jesus died for.

I don't struggle with TV as much as I struggle with movies. I'm too easily entertained, so one of the things I've done in recent years is let my wife decide if I should see a movie or not. Her filter is better than mine, so she gets online and looks at the reviews. If it's not something she wants me to see, then I don't see it.

A few years ago I took my son and daughter to see the Disney movie *Frozen*. About halfway through it, Silas leaned over to me and said, "There isn't a boy on the planet who will make the mistake of seeing this twice!"

My daughter doesn't share my son's opinion on that movie.

But weeding out the bad stuff isn't enough. I also have to water the good stuff in my life. On that front I have always lived by a simple principle: pay now, play later.

I was at a fund-raiser a few weeks ago for a hospital that takes care of stroke victims. A good friend of mine leaned over during the dinner and said, "We pay now for what we might need later in life."

That is a great principle to apply to our character development. We invest in our hearts *now*, because when the going gets tough *later*, we'll be glad we developed a strong root system to weather the storm.

"No discipline seems pleasant at the time, but painful. Later on, however, it produces a harvest of righteousness and peace for those who have been trained by it" (Heb. 12:11 NIV).

Jesus didn't promise us an easy life. He promised us a better life. And the only way we will experience the better life is by allowing Jesus to discipline us. One of the ways I keep my mind focused on the benefits associated with discipline is through memorizing and meditating on God's Word.

Good athletes have good mechanics. When no one was looking, Tony Gwynn hit hundreds of baseballs in the same way that Larry Bird took hundreds of jump shots. Behind the scenes they mastered the fundamentals of their respective sports through repetition, and in the heat of competition, when millions of people were watching them, the practice paid off. They made what few of us can do look easy.

If we start our day by downloading information about sports or politics or fashion, then we will think about sports, politics, or fashion throughout the day. What we feed our brains early in the morning is what we'll think about the rest of the day.

What if the first minutes of our day were spent memorizing God's Word, and the rest of the day was spent meditating on what we memorized? The more I memorize and meditate, the more satisfied my appetites are.

I struggle with contentment, so in recent months I've memorized several verses about the peace of God. And during that stretch of time, God has pruned my life by showing me just how materialistic I am. I have learned how my materialistic pursuits will never give me what I want, which is a settled peace.

He's also putting me in conversations with other people who are hungry for contentment. Through our honest dialogue, I'm realizing the fruit that is hanging on the branches of my life doesn't just benefit me. The fruit was meant to feed other people too.

My grandparents farmed thousands of acres of wheat and corn in western Kansas, but they didn't do the work alone. They were sharecroppers, which means they partnered with other farmers to plow, plant, cultivate, and harvest their food. As farmers, they learned there is strength in numbers because they were able to share best and worst practices with people who were tilling similar soil.

There is wisdom in cooperation. The fruit hanging on the branches of your life wasn't meant to feed just you, but everyone you know. Everyone you know will benefit from the hard work God is doing in your life.

Ubuntu is a word that South Africans use, and from what I understand, it's several words condensed into one. The meaning is fascinating. Ubuntu means "a person is a person through other persons."

We were created for community. Each of us needs the rest of us. When your roots and my roots grow together, every part of our lives gets stronger. Nothing can knock us over if we link arms and farm together.

I call it spiritual sharecropping.

Let's learn from each other. I want to learn what Jesus has taught you about marriage, parenting, and finances. I want to know what to do and what not to do. I never want to stop learning because Jesus has so much to teach me. And I'm convinced some of the lessons I need to learn will come from you. I'm full of questions, such as:

How did you become so patient?

How did you develop self-control?

How did you learn to be gentle?

The fruit that I see in your life is the fruit I want in my life. So let's learn from one another. Decide today that you're going to start asking questions of the people around you whose lives are bearing healthy fruit. Ask them to help you identify the things that threaten what Jesus wants to grow in your life.

One of the things that I'm seeing in our country today is a lack of intentional conversation about character development. When I hear about a dad throwing his daughter off a bridge, or mobs of people beating people up for fun in a mall, what I connect that to is a lack of character formation at an early age, and daily erosion of the heart's fertile soil.

I'm a visual learner, so the picture that comes to my mind is of the Kansas dust bowl in the 1930s—the dirty thirties, when a once-fertile land with an abundance of crops became a wasteland that wouldn't take seed of any kind. I don't want that image to be what I think of when I consider the condition of the human heart in our country, but that is what comes to mind based on the behavior I'm seeing.

One of the best ways to learn from Jesus is to learn from each other. Let's be intentional about spiritual sharecropping because farming is hard work, but the load is lightened when we share the responsibility.

I went to lunch recently with two businessmen who wanted to enter into an accountability relationship with each other, but they weren't sure how to do it. Both are successful in their respective occupations but wanted to be more successful as husbands and dads. I shared with them what I've learned from my accountability partners, which is: the more vulnerable you are, the more you will grow.

Someone needs to know about the weeds that threaten the seeds Jesus has planted in you. I have friends who know that I struggle with pride, lust, and greed. Those weeds threaten to kill everything Jesus wants to grow in me.

That's why Jesus explained his parable about the seed and soil this way:

> "Now listen to the explanation of the parable about the farmer planting seeds: The seed that fell on the footpath represents those who hear the message about the Kingdom and don't understand it. Then the evil one comes and snatches away the seed that was planted in their hearts. The seed on the rocky soil represents those who hear the message and immediately receive it with joy. But since they don't have deep roots, they don't last long. They fall away as soon as they have problems or are persecuted for believing God's word. The seed that fell among the thorns represents those who hear God's word, but all too quickly the message is crowded out by the worries of this life and the lure of wealth, so no fruit is produced. The seed that fell on good soil represents those who truly hear and understand God's word and produce a harvest of thirty, sixty, or even a hundred times as much as had been planted!" (Matt. 13:18–23 NLT)

I want that for you! I want your life to produce so much fruit that people from all over come to hear about how God grew things in your life that you never thought possible.

Farming is hard, dirty work. You cannot do it alone. So look for some other people with dirt under their fingernails and invite them into the garden of your heart.

PART 2

THE CHURCH—WHAT JESUS IS DOING

THE FIRST DAY OF THE WEEK IS MY FAVORITE DAY OF THE WEEK.

I love watching people walk through the doors of our church campuses on Sunday. Tall people and short people, old people and young people, rich people and poor people file in and find a seat. No two people look the same because no two people are the same.

We sit and stand. We laugh and cry. We sing and say nothing. Church is a study in contrast, as it should be.

Church is where we learn that salvation is greater than sin and life is greater than death. It's where we hear a message that what we see isn't all there is.

The church is the body of Christ. The church is Jesus on earth.

So when people ask, "Where is God?" we point to God's people and say, "He's with them, and they're with him." God chose to live in his people, so wherever his people go is where he is.

The church is mobile and global.

I've been in churches where the people speak Chinese, Spanish, German, Arabic, and English. I've been in churches that meet in tents, theaters, warehouses, living rooms, gymnasiums, and under trees outside. No two churches are the same. Instead of arguing about our differences, we should celebrate the differences.

The church doesn't always agree about everything, but we do always love each other. And not only do we love one another, but we also love everyone.

The church is for everyone everywhere. No matter who you are, what you've done, you belong with God's people. We're not better than anyone. We're just different.

With your permission, that is what we're going to explore in these chapters.

8

INCLUSIVITY: FROM CRUMBS TO COMMUNION

HAVE YOU EVER SAID SOMETHING YOU WISH YOU COULD TAKE BACK?

When I moved from Haiti to Kentucky, I went to the DMV because I needed a new driver's license. If a person were to rob me at gunpoint today, I'd give them all my cash and credit cards but would ask to keep my driver's license because I'm scared of the people who work at the DMV!

When I finally got to the front of the line, the woman behind the counter asked me for my paperwork.

"How are you doing today?" I asked.

"As good as can be expected when you work at the DMV!" she said, not smiling. "And you?"

"Well, ma'am, I'm a little nervous," I said, "because I always get down here and have the wrong paperwork."

She looked at my paperwork, and without looking at me, she said, "You should be nervous, but not because you have the wrong papers. You should be nervous because you called me ma'am, and I'm a man!"

There is no recovering from that! I had just put my foot in my mouth and swallowed it.

Most of us can remember the dumb things we've said over the years, but few of us can recall the moments when we said the right thing at the right time.

Jesus had a conversation with a woman who said the right thing at the right time. To understand why her statement was so profound, we have to understand how divided men and women were, how divided Jews and Gentiles were.

In the Talmud is a prayer that Jewish men prayed on a regular basis: "Blessed are you, Lord, our God, ruler of the universe, who has not created me a woman." In other prayer literature we learn they frequently prayed, "Father, thank you for not making me a Gentile, a slave, or a woman."

Needless to say, there was a gender gap and an ethnic gap that existed in the world Jesus lived in. And this was never more apparent than at a meal. What united people in antiquity was food. If someone was seated at your table, they were your friend.

If they were never invited to share a meal in your home, they were an enemy. Men ate with men. Women ate with women. Jews ate with Jews. Gentiles ate with Gentiles. But they never ate together.

The word people used to describe an enemy was *dog*. Dogs were not pets in the ancient world, but rather scavenging animals that typically took up residence on trash heaps outside the city limits. There they would fight with other dogs for scraps of food.

Jesus entered into a discussion with religious leaders about dietary laws. In the course of the conversation the religious leaders accused Jesus' disciples of not washing their hands. This accusation was serious, carrying with it far more grave consequences than spreading germs. Unclean hands were not permitted to worship a holy God, and there were spiritual ramifications for not washing one's hands before eating a meal.

Jesus wanted to know: Were unclean hands worse than unclean hearts? He had an uncanny way of deconstructing the arrogant attacks of the religious elite. When Jesus declared all foods to be clean, it created quite the murmur among the crowd.

"If he can declare all food to be clean, does that mean he can declare all people to be clean too?"

On the heels of this controversial conversation, Jesus left Israel for the first time in his ministry and traveled to Tyre. Tyre was a seaport town on the Mediterranean Sea where merchants would let their hair down and put their feet up. It was the Gentile version of Las Vegas. Weary sailors would indulge in all things sinful.

What happened in Tyre stayed in Tyre.

No Jew of good reputation would get within eyesight of this city, let alone dare to step foot in it. Jesus not only dared to go there, he engaged a Gentile woman in conversation. And not just any woman, but a woman whose daughter had an evil spirit living in her.

To recap: Jesus was in an unclean city, having a conversation with an unclean woman, whose daughter had an unclean spirit. This might be the most scandalous conversation recorded for us in the New Testament.

The Gentile woman asked Jesus to heal her daughter.

"First I should feed the children—my own family, the Jews," Jesus responded. "It isn't right to take food from the children and throw it to the dogs" (Mark 7:27 NLT).

Jesus acknowledged the gender and ethnic gap existing between her and him, but I don't think he wanted to widen the gap. I think he wanted to bridge it. Jesus came to bring salvation to all people, "the Jew first and also the Gentile" (Rom. 1:16 NLT). The sequence doesn't indicate favoritism, but function.

If you invited all your friends to be at your house for a Super Bowl party by 5:00 p.m., but you had a friend show up at 4:00 p.m., you wouldn't ask them to stand outside until the party started. You would invite that person in because they were invited to the party.

This Gentile woman showed up to God's party ahead of time, but she seemed to understand she'd been invited. She seemed to know that sequence didn't indicate favoritism, but function.

"That's true, Lord," she replied, "but even the dogs under the table are allowed to eat the scraps from the children's plates" (Mark 7:28 NLT).

A family's meal didn't need to be interrupted and the children's nourishment didn't need to suffer in order for a dog to receive a crumb. She knew Jesus could help the Gentiles without it hurting the Jews. She not only understood who Jesus was. She also understood why he came into the world.

And Jesus is impressed.

"Good answer!" he said. "Now go home, for the demon has left your daughter" (Mark 7:29 NLT).

As scandalous as this interaction was back then, it loses its shock value on us because we're not living amid the same social tension. Even so, we can see the point: Jesus invites people under the table to sit at the table. If a person was willing to eat with Jesus, Jesus was willing to eat with them.

I've tried to picture what Jesus' dining room table would look like and whom he would invite to share a meal with him. Can't you see him sitting between Hitler and Einstein? A man who wanted to rid the world of Jewish people and a brilliant Jewish man who contributed so much to the world. Can you imagine the headlines on CNN after that meal?

Or, I could see Jesus setting the table for a breakfast conversation with Governor George Wallace and Martin Luther King Jr.—a racist politician from the Deep South and the leader of the civil rights movement.

Pick the most unlikely people to share a meal together, and Jesus would invite them to sit at his table.

"Treat other people *exactly* as you would like to be treated" (Matt. 7:12 PHILLIPS, emphasis mine).

I struggle with that verse because I understand that verse.

If Jesus invited me to his house for dinner and told me he had also invited a group of terrorists to join us, I would struggle to show up.

I'm not a racist. I'm not a sexist. But I struggle to treat terrorists as I would like to be treated. I struggle to love men who hurt women and children. I struggle to love men who use religion as a means to hurt instead of help people.

"Love your enemies!" Jesus said. "Pray for those who persecute you!" (Matt. 5:44 NLT). Jesus knew if we would pray for our enemies, God would help us love our enemies. I haven't prayed for ISIS, but I need to. If I don't pray for my enemies, I'll never be able to eat with them.

I've noticed this about myself. I have both an instinctive response and a reflective response to people who irritate me. When someone cuts me off in traffic, my instinctive response is to honk my horn and throw my hands up in the air. However, my reflective response says, "Maybe they had a hard day at work, or maybe there's a child in the backseat who distracted them."

Jesus is inviting us to trade our instinctive responses for reflective responses. Doing so can impact how we treat people. It teaches us to never judge an entire people group based on the actions of a few people in that group.

As the reflective followers of Jesus, we would never say, "All women are emotional basket cases and all men are insensitive jerks," because that isn't true. Some are, but some aren't.

As the reflective followers of Jesus, we would never say, "All priests are predators, all politicians are corrupt, and all law enforcement officers are heavy-handed." I have friends who are priests, politicians, and police officers, and most of them are great people.

As the reflective followers of Jesus, we would never say, "All black people are unmotivated, all Hispanic people are here illegally, and all middle-aged white men are greedy bigots," because that just isn't true.

We should never judge an entire group of people based on the actions of a few people in that group.

In the field of psychology there is an emotional axiom called transference, wherein we transfer how we feel about Person A onto Person B, who reminds us of Person A. Say you had a bad relationship with your mom growing up. If later in life you meet someone who looks like or acts like your mom, you might transfer how you feel about your mom onto that person.

Fortunately, God has transferred how he feels about Jesus onto us. Because he loves Jesus, he loves us. And in response, he asks us to transfer the love we've received from him to everyone we meet.

The Bible calls this transfer of love *grace*.

Justice is getting what I deserve. Mercy is not getting what I deserve. Grace is getting what I don't deserve. Jesus is God's picture of grace because he doesn't treat us as our sins deserve. Instead he gives us what we don't deserve, which is grace.

Because of grace, I'm convinced that if Jesus were alive today, he would spend the majority of his time in prisons and rehabs. I think he would feel right at home at an AA meeting. If I close my eyes, I can see Jesus sitting on the front row of a divorce court or on the curb outside a strip club. I imagine him walking through the hallways of an inner-city high school or a frat house or a nursing home. What's funny to me is that when I picture Jesus in my mind, I never picture him in a church building.

Once I heard a man struggling with homosexuality say, "It's easier to get sex on the street than a hug in a church." I want to invite him to the church where I serve because he could find thousands of people who are willing to hug him. And the reason we would embrace him is because of grace.

We were once under the table, but Jesus invited us to sit at the table. We were once enemies of God, but Jesus made us his friends.

"See to it that *no one* falls short of the grace of God" (Heb. 12:15 NIV, emphasis mine).

I receive grace more easily than I give it away. I want to love my enemies, and I want to treat people exactly as I want to be treated. I want to make sure no one misses out on the grace of God. But my actions don't always reflect my intentions.

Jesus always practiced what he preached. When the people who crucified him mocked him, he said, "Father, forgive them, for they do not know what they do" (Luke 23:34). He didn't have enemies because Jesus loved the people who hated him.

At the heart of this story about an unclean woman from an unclean city is an all-important truth: No matter who you are, you matter to Jesus. He doesn't want to pay you back for the wrong you've done; he wants to bring you back, so he's prepared a place for you at his table.

I'm convinced heaven will be filled with people who struggled to get along here on earth. But with Jesus at the table, they won't struggle to get along anymore. I'm learning that if I don't put Jesus between me and my enemies, I won't be able to love them.

My enemy is no different from me. I need the same amount of grace my enemy needs. Acknowledging this helps me love them.

Bill Moyers produced a documentary for PBS on the famous hymn "Amazing Grace." The song was written by John Newton, a violent slave trader who experienced the love of God during a storm on his merchant ship. The storm nearly capsized Newton's ship, but God rescued him and his crew, causing Newton to slowly turn his life over to God. He later joined William Wilberforce's fight to end slavery in the civilized world. Newton was a slave trader turned slave liberator.

The documentary features a 1988 concert that took place at Wembley Stadium in London to raise money for Nelson Mandela and his fight against apartheid in South Africa. Several million people watched the concert on television while thousands more witnessed it in person. Bands including U2 and the Rolling Stones worked the crowd into a frenzy, and by the time Guns N' Roses took the stage, the scene had turned dangerously chaotic as most people in attendance were either drunk or high.

Jessye Norman, a famous African American opera singer, was the last performer of the night. Without the accompaniment of a band, she stepped up to the microphone and began to sing,

"Amazing grace, how sweet the sound that saved a wretch like me! I once was lost but now am found—was blind, but now I see."[1]

By the end of the second verse, a solemn silence fell on the rowdy crowd. And by the end of the third verse, thousands of people were singing with her. It's as if the crowd realized the power of a song that, when sung in public, draws people out of their intoxicated stupor and grounds them in a humble sobriety. By the end of the song, an entire stadium of people was singing about what the world really needs and what the world really lacks. In the documentary Moyers interviews Norman, whose rendition of "Amazing Grace" creates a powerful juxtaposition when you consider that her ancestors were once slaves.

Grace. It's what my enemies and I need.

What unites those of us who know Jesus is this: that we deserve crumbs, but we get Communion. Jesus does not treat us as we deserve to be treated, so how can we treat anyone differently?

OPPORTUNITY: A DAD WHO UNDERSTANDS MOMS

I WAS THIRTEEN, WORKING ON SOME HOMEWORK AT THE KITCHEN TABLE, when the yellow crank-dial phone that hung on the wall rang. My mom was washing dishes at the time, and I remember her gently drying off her hands before she answered it.

"Oh no!" was her response. I watched as her shoulders sank and her hand moved to cover her open mouth. "Oh no! Oh no! Oh no!" she repeated, shaking her head. Whoever she was talking to and whatever she was talking about wasn't good.

A few minutes later, she slowly hung up the phone and turned to me with tears in her eyes.

"Sam took his own life," she said.

My good friend—the right fielder on our summer baseball team, the boy with a quick wit—got off the bus, ate a snack, then made his way to the basement of his house where he ended his life.

No note. No explanation. Nothing but shock.

I remember going to the funeral home with classmates. As I sat near the back of the room, the quiet was interrupted by the sound of an occasional sniffle. Everyone watched as Sam's mom leaned on the casket, her legs buckling under the emotional weight of it.

Forty thousand people will take their own lives this year in our country. Another three million people will try but fail. Suicide is the tenth leading cause of death among adults, the second leading cause of death for ages 10–24, and sadly, the third leading cause of death among college students. One in every twelve college students will attempt to end their life.[1]

"Why do people commit suicide?" my daughter asked me recently.

"Some people do it because they are committed to a cause," I explained. I told her about the followers of Heaven's Gate, the Branch Davidians, the 913 followers of Jim Jones, as well as suicide bombers committed to sacrificing their lives for jihad. "For others," I continued, "it's a long, painful battle with a chronic illness. After years of aches and pains, lying on their back or being confined to a wheelchair, they throw in the towel."

For many senior adults, loneliness leads them to take their life. A loved one has passed on, and they can't stomach the thought of spending another holiday isolated in their house or in a nursing home.

For some teenagers, it's a cry for attention. The music they listen to and the movies they watch may glamorize suicide, lionizing the person who takes their own life.

The list of reasons is long. But the reality is that depression is the leading cause of suicide in the United States. Ninety percent of all suicides are depression related.

"Hope deferred makes the heart sick" (Prov. 13:12).

We all deal with sadness in our lives from time to time; we all battle mood swings, and we all have our weak moments. But not all of us have a chemical imbalance in our bodies that causes us to believe there is no light at the end of the tunnel, no reason to get out of bed. Sadly, many people don't know about the great combination of prayer and pills to help them deal with the hopeless feeling that the sun is never going to shine again.

Add to the misery a very real enemy who attacks and taunts and accuses and whispers, "You won't be missed. No one cares about you. No one loves you."

Jesus said of Satan, "The thief does not come except to steal, and to kill, and to destroy" (John 10:10). Satan has only *one* purpose, which is to steal, kill, and destroy you and me. He will steal our sense of value and convince us that life is pointless. He will kill us by confusing us to the point that we die emotionally long before we grab a bottle of pills or a handgun.

And "destroy"—isn't that what suicide does? It destroys hope for those who take their lives, and for the family members left behind.

"He was a murderer from the beginning," Jesus also said of Satan, "not holding to the truth, for there is no truth in him. When he lies, he speaks his native language, for he is a liar and the father of lies" (John 8:44 NIV). Satan convinces people that dying is better than living, when in reality suicide doesn't solve or simplify the problem. It only complicates and compounds the problem.

Our enemy is real and subtle, and unfortunately he has impeccable timing. He knows what to say, when to say it, and most importantly, to whom to say it.

Larry was one of those people. Satan had his ear and his undivided attention.

I had to tell Larry's middle school- and his high school–aged sons that their dad had ended his life. They walked into the living room after football practice, and the minute they saw me sitting on the couch, one of them ran outside. The other son shook his head and said, "He finally did it, didn't he?" They knew.

Their dad had lost his job months earlier, and they'd watched him spiral into a deep, dark pit of despair. His identity as a man was defined by his job and the paycheck it provided, so when the job was taken away, his reason for living went with it.

The morning after breaking the news to them, I found myself sitting in the bedroom of the youngest son. A picture of his baseball team sat nearby. His dad had been his coach.

"Is my dad in heaven or hell?" he asked me. His voice was barely audible.

"I don't get to decide that. That's between God and your dad," I said.

"Someone told my mom that suicide is unforgivable. Is that true?" he asked.

"The Bible doesn't say that," I responded. "I'm sorry someone said that to your mom."

Suicide is sinful. The Bible clearly teaches that God has numbered our days, and when we cut those days short, we circumvent the plan of God. To commit suicide is to murder oneself, violating the sixth commandment in the process.

"It's my life!" some say. "I can do what I want!"

"You are not your own; you were bought at a price. Therefore honor God with your bodies" (1 Cor. 6:19–20 NIV).

Suicide limits the power of God. When a person takes their own life, they are boldly declaring, "My problem is bigger than God's power." And that is never true.

Like all sin, suicide breaks the heart of God. But is it unforgivable? Let's explore that.

There are six suicides mentioned in the pages of the Bible, but none of them is referred to as an "unforgivable" sin. The most infamous suicide in the Bible is that of Judas. When talking about his betrayal, Jesus said of Judas, "It would have been good for that man if he had not been born" (Matt. 26:24). I've been in church services and funerals where that one verse is used to declare that all who commit suicide go immediately to hell.

But Jesus didn't say that.

Could it be that Jesus was looking ahead, knowing full well that Judas would not repent, that Judas would die without salvation, and that in going to hell, it would've been better if he had not been born in the first place? Could it be that Jesus actually made this statement with heartache in his voice?

Anything else would be inconsistent with the ministry of Jesus, the teaching of Jesus, and the salvation that Jesus came to freely give to all people.

Maybe Judas didn't go to hell because he committed suicide. Maybe he committed suicide because he was going to hell.

God doesn't judge us based on the worst decision we make in life, but on the best decision we make in life. And that is to let Jesus save us. And what does Jesus save us from?

Sin. All sin. Including suicide.

"For I am convinced that neither *death* nor life, neither angels nor demons, neither the present nor the future, nor any powers, neither height nor depth, nor *anything else* in *all* creation, will be able to separate us from the love of God that is in Christ Jesus our Lord" (Rom. 8:38–39 NIV, emphasis mine).

Jesus experienced an emotional low in his life and reached the conclusion in the Garden of Gethsemane that dying would be better than living, saying, "My soul is overwhelmed with sorrow to the point of death" (Matt. 26:38 NIV).

That is a sadness I've never experienced in my life.

The apostle Paul found the bottom of the barrel as well. He wrote, "We were under great pressure, far beyond our ability to endure, so that we despaired of life itself" (2 Cor. 1:8 NIV).

But neither of them committed suicide. Paul and Jesus reached the same conclusion: Suicide doesn't eliminate pain. Suicide creates more pain.

I can validate that, as a person left behind to deal with the family members of those who take their lives and the questions and the confusion suicide creates. So if you or someone you know is struggling with loneliness, sadness, depression, or thoughts of suicide, I want you to know that help and hope are available.

"Is anyone crying for help? God is listening, ready to rescue you. If your heart is broken, you'll find God right there; if you're kicked in the gut, he'll help you catch your breath" (Ps. 34:17–18 msg).

You can run to God.

"God is our refuge and strength, a very present help in trouble" (Ps. 46:1).

I have a friend named Jamie, and he started this incredible online movement called "To Write Love on Her Arms." He helps struggling people understand that no one else can play their parts in the story that God is writing.

Jamie is a "me too" leader. He refuses to let anyone believe their life doesn't matter. After a famous comedian took his life, Jamie wrote these powerful words:

> If you feel too much, there's still a place for you here.
> If you feel too much, don't go.
> If this world is too painful, stop and rest.
> It's okay to stop and rest.
> If you need a break, it's okay to say you need a break.
> This life—it's not a contest, not a race, not a performance, not a thing that you win.
> It's okay to slow down.

91

*You are here for more than grades, more than a job, more than
	a promotion, more than keeping up, more than getting by.*
This life is not about status or opinion or appearance.
You don't have to fake it.
You do not have to fake it.
Other people feel this way too.
If your heart is broken, it's okay to say your heart is broken.
If you feel stuck, it's okay to say you feel stuck.
If you can't let go, it's okay to say you can't let go.
You are not alone in these places.
Other people feel how you feel.
*You are more than just your pain. You are more than wounds,
	more than drugs, more than death and silence.*
There is still some time to be surprised.
There is still some time to ask for help.
There is still some time to start again.
There is still some time for love to find you.
It's not too late.
You're not alone.
*It's okay—whatever you need and however long it takes—it's
	okay.*
It's okay.
If you feel too much, there's still a place for you here.
If you feel too much, don't go.
There is still some time.[2]

Suicidal thoughts might provide the greatest "me too"
opportunity for us to love people where they are and as they are.
God wants us to lighten people's emotional loads: "Bear one
another's burdens, and so fulfill the law of Christ" (Gal. 6:2).

Shared joy is double joy, but shared pain is half pain.

In the aftermath of my friend's suicide, I wish I knew what I know now. No one knew what to say at his funeral or to his parents. I would want Mrs. Reily to know that God is a dad who understands moms.

He feels your pain.

10

INTEGRITY: CROOKED LINES

SPANX IS A PRODUCT THAT PROMISES TO MAKE US LOOK SKINNIER THAN we are. If you read the back of the box, Spanx claims it can hide the fat we don't want the world to know we have. The actual wording is "firms chest, narrows waistline, and flattens stomach."

Who can live without Spanx? Not me!

I bought the T-shirt version of Spanx and took it home to try it out. As I pulled it out of the box, I thought, *This might fit my eleven-year-old son.* But I was so enamored with the idea of getting my youthful physique back without having to exercise that I put it on.

Aside from trying to drink an entire gallon of milk in ten minutes at a middle school camp, putting on Spanx was the worst decision of my life. I almost had to go to the emergency room to have the shirt cut off! Nowhere in the fine print did it say that suffocation was possible, but I'm pretty sure I cracked some ribs.

Over the years, I've learned there are some things we cannot hide. What is inside us is going to come out of us.

I have a good friend named Grace Anna who has a rare form of scoliosis crushing her spine. Her condition adversely affects her ability to breathe. It has also stunted her growth, caused blindness, and impaired her ability to hear. Needless to say, her life is no picnic in the park.

But Grace Anna loves Jesus, and the joy Jesus has planted in her life comes out of her in the form of song. She has become a bit of a celebrity on YouTube and Facebook. Hundreds of thousands of people have been inspired by her ability to sing in spite of her circumstances.

"At the cross, at the cross, where I first saw the light," she sings with a southern twang, "and the burden of my heart rolled away. It was there by faith I received my sight and now I am happy all the day."[1]

The first time I saw her sing in person, I couldn't stop crying. I was so happy I cried. Have you ever been so happy you cried?

I know for many people the phrase "tears of joy" is an oxymoron. We don't naturally associate tears with joy. But when I think of an oxymoron, I think of pairs of words that don't go together—like *jumbo shrimp* or *Cubs win*.

ME TOO

An oxymoron is a figure of speech in which apparently contradictory terms appear in conjunction. Shrimp are small, and the Cubs haven't won a World Series since 1908. I have friends who think *country music* is an oxymoron, but I don't agree with them.

In the Jewish community where Jesus was raised, putting the words *savior* and *sinner* in the same sentence, let alone in the same room, was a spiritual contradiction of the highest degree.

In that regard, Jesus steered his life toward contradiction.

While eating in the home of a wealthy man named Simon, Jesus was approached by a prostitute who kissed his dirty feet and washed them with her tears and hair. In the first century, a woman became a prostitute because her parents sold her to pay off a debt, or her husband died from a sickness or was killed in a war. Most women who became prostitutes didn't want to be prostitutes.

This much is certain about this woman: She knew who she was, and she knew who Jesus was. She was a sinner, and Jesus was a Savior. And I'm sure people nearly choked on their food as they watched her take the bobby pins out of her hair. Joel Green, a New Testament scholar, noted, "Letting her hair down in this setting would have been on a par with appearing topless in public (today)."[2]

Men and women did not interact like this in public, let alone a prophet and a prostitute. But I bet this was not her first interaction with Jesus. She had either heard him teach publicly or talked with him privately. Either way, she was so happy she cried.

What was inside her came out of her.

Years of sadness and shame dripped from her eyes onto Jesus' feet in a steady stream of relief. She didn't care what anyone else thought of her because she knew what Jesus thought of her.

To contextualize this, imagine inviting Jesus to your house for dinner, and halfway through the meal, Heidi Fleiss or Monica Lewinsky or Lindsay Lohan or anyone else with a big black book and a public sexual history rings your doorbell and wants to pull up a chair next to your honored guest.

You would be shocked. You would be stunned. You would be speechless.

There is an axiom in the realm of philosophy that says, "You won't know a crooked line is crooked unless you have a straight line to compare it to." Jesus is the straight line. And every person who stands in his presence quickly realizes just how crooked their life is.

After parting ways with the Beatles, John Lennon moved to New York City. Due to his worldwide fame, he was forced to stay inside his apartment. His preferred way to pass time was to watch television. And to the surprise of many, one of his favorite things to watch was a Billy Graham Crusade. It led him to write letters to Graham and other evangelical leaders. In one letter to Oral Roberts, Lennon wrote: "Money can't buy me love. It's true. The point is this, I want happiness. I don't want to keep on with drugs . . . Explain to me what Christianity can do for me. Is it phoney? Can (Jesus) love me? I want out of hell."[3]

Fellow musician and recent convert Bob Dylan explained to Lennon that not only could Jesus love him, but also that Jesus did love him.

I'm sure there are some people who would be surprised if they saw Jesus and John Lennon eating dinner together. In the same way, Simon was left scratching his head as he watched Jesus allow an immoral woman to wash his feet with her hair.

That's why Jesus told Simon, "Look at this woman kneeling here" (Luke 7:44 NLT). All Simon could see when he looked at this woman was her sin, but Jesus wanted Simon to see *her*. She was a person. She had a name. She was created in the image of God. Jesus was going to die for her. Jesus was going to straighten out her crooked life.

When I lived in Haiti, I had a friend named Esther who was crippled. Her legs were bent at a weird angle, making it difficult to walk. The first time I saw her, I felt sorry for her. When I learned that she was a prostitute, I asked Jesus to help me love her.

From time to time, she would come to my house in need of food, medicine, or money. It seemed as though every time I saw her, she was pregnant. I knew I couldn't convince men to stop taking advantage of her, so I decided to show her that not all men are animals. I wanted her to know that she didn't have to crawl into bed with men to be loved by them.

After several interactions with her, I invited her to church. She politely declined my invitation. "No one at church wants to see me," she would say, with sadness in her voice.

"That's not true," I would say, smiling. "I want to see you there! Jesus wants to see you there!"

She never came.

Few things sadden me more than knowing Esther believes that Jesus sees her the way the world sees her.

In a world that celebrates the abuse of women through the sale of books and movies like *Fifty Shades of Grey*, we need to be reminded that we follow a God who loves women and sees them as the beautiful and divine image bearers that they are.

A "me too" culture is one of equality where men and women celebrate their differences and similarities with radical love and joy.

"For *all* have sinned and fall short of the glory of God" (Rom. 3:23, emphasis mine).

We've all sinned and we've all fallen. But we don't feel the same. Some of us measure how far we've fallen and compare it to how far we think others have fallen. Some of us feel as though we haven't fallen as far as others have, while others of us feel as though we have fallen farther.

Jesus doesn't measure the distance. He bridges the distance.

That's why Jesus told Simon, "I tell you, her sins—and they are many—have been forgiven, so she has shown me much love. But a person who is forgiven little shows only little love" (Luke 7:47 NLT).

The important truth surfacing at Simon's house was that making mistakes was better than faking perfection.

I am so far from being perfect that I couldn't fake it if I tried. If you give me a list of all the sins listed in the Bible, I could check every box. Pride? I've got boatloads of it. Lust? Like every man on the planet, I wrestle with it. Greed? Jealousy? Anger? I can check every box that you can check.

But like me and the prostitute who soaked Jesus' feet, you are totally forgiven. When Jesus looks at you, he doesn't see your sin at all. He sees you! You don't have to be perfect because he already is, and his perfection is enough.

And that makes me so happy I could cry.

When my daughter was little, we would play a game when I came home from work. I would say, "Ava, do I love you this much?" And I would separate my hands a few inches from one another.

"No, Daddy," she would say, giggling. "You love me more!"

So I would separate my hands a little bit more and ask, "How about this much?"

"Daddy, more! Much more!" she would say with excitement.

As I stretched out my arms as far as they could possibly go, Ava would run and wrap her little arms around my legs. I would pick her up and squeeze her and hug her and kiss her and tell her that I loved her more than she could ever know.

Not everyone in the world understands the expansive love the Father has for us, his kids.

I was signing books at a bookstore recently when a man walked by. Based on the angry look on his face, I thought he was either going to knock all the books off the table or knock me out.

He didn't do either, but through clenched teeth he did say, "I would never buy *that* book!" He was referring to the last book I wrote.

As I sat there the rest of the evening, interacting with so many gracious and kind people, I couldn't help but think about that one man. Who hurt him? Who made him so angry and mean that he lashed out at a total stranger?

My dog Charlie is a bit skittish. If you make a loud sound or drop something on the floor, he runs and hides.

A lot of people are like that. They've been conditioned to be scared or mean. They either hide from people or they hurt people.

The woman who was so happy she cried in the presence of Jesus could have spent the rest of her life hiding from people or hurting people. Instead she chose to let Jesus heal her. And I think that's why she cried so hard.

When you've been hiding and hurting for so long and you suddenly realize healing is possible, you can't help but shed a tear. It's okay to cry, but some people think they need permission. We have tear ducts for a reason. And we need to use them more than we do.

If your job is draining you, if your kids aren't listening to you, if your husband cheated on you, if your parents neglected you, if you're being picked on at school, make your way to Jesus and let it out. What is inside you needs to come out.

Jesus will be honored by your humility, and he'll honor you for your humility.

If nothing else, don't be like Simon. He lived a life that was buttoned up and bottled up. Like many religious people in his day, he faked perfection, and on many levels, that's worse than being a prostitute.

It's impossible to straighten out a line that doesn't know it's crooked.

RESPONSIBILITY: BABY POWDER

MY KIDS RECENTLY WATCHED THE MOVIE *NIGHT AT THE MUSEUM*, WHICH made them really want to go to Washington, DC. So we loaded up, drove to Washington, and took in all of the incredible sites our nation's capitol has to offer. What I loved about the trip was that everywhere we went, the kids didn't say, "Wow, George Washington sat here," or, "Wow, Thomas Jefferson stood there."

No, in a tour of the Smithsonian, my son asked the guide, "Is this where Ben Stiller chased the monkey?"

The older gentleman, who had been trained to answer any and all questions about the Smithsonian, locked up. He didn't know what to say.

Have you ever been in a similar situation? Someone says something or asks something that you're not expecting, and the connection between your brain and mouth feels momentarily unplugged?

Last summer I had the same dream every night for a month. In the dream, a young woman was seated outside my office crying. When I asked her what was wrong, she said, "I've had an abortion."

As I pulled up a chair across from her, she always said the same two things: "I don't think God could ever forgive me," and, "Why didn't anyone tell me it would hurt this much?"

Every night I woke up at the same time, not really knowing what to do with the dream. And after a month of lying in my bed in silence, what I heard God saying to me was, "Please say something."

Because abortion has become a politically charged subject, lines have been drawn. When I listen to what everyone else is saying, what I hear them saying is this: pro-life is pro-baby, and pro-choice is pro-woman. I hear them saying that one group champions and protects the rights of babies while the other group champions and protects the rights of women.

And on some level we're forced to pick a side; it's an either/or proposition.

The problem is this: our leader, Jesus, is both/and. Jesus is pro-baby and pro-woman.

Jesus was born to a scandalous, teenage mom. When you read about Jesus' life, you get the impression that at some point his mom sat him down and shared with him all the public humiliation and fear she experienced as a young, unwed, pregnant woman. It seems to have shaped Jesus' ministry because Jesus publicly, demonstratively loved children and women and elevated their value in first-century society.

There are so many women suffering in silence each weekend in churches across America because they don't know what to do with the shame they're carrying.

A woman was pulled out of bed where she was having an affair with a married man. Religious leaders threw her at the feet of Jesus. Naked, heart pounding, palms sweating, she couldn't look up. The shame was too heavy. That's when the mob posed a question to Jesus: "What do You say?" (John 8:5).

When I don't know what to say, I look to see what Jesus had to say. He didn't say anything at first. Instead, he knelt down and began to write in the dirt with his finger.

We don't know what he wrote, but my best guess is he wrote the names of the men who were holding rocks. Maybe next to their names he named their sins—the sins they deserved to die for. And the reason I believe that is because of what he said next.

"Let any one of you who is without sin be the first to throw a stone at her" (John 8:7 NIV).

The crowd went silent. All that could be heard that day was the sound of rocks hitting the ground. One by one, the men left.

Some would say that Jesus wrote in the sand to prove a point to the angry crowd. I believe he wrote in the sand so he could look the woman in the eyes.

Jesus, a loving man, sat face-to-face with a wounded woman.

"Woman, where are they? Has no one condemned you?"

"No one, sir," she said.

"Then neither do I condemn you," Jesus declared. "Go now and leave your life of sin" (John 8:10–11 NIV).

Like men, women fall into one of two categories with Jesus. Women are either forgiven or forgivable. Anyone who has been shamed by sexual sin is forgivable. If you are a follower of Jesus, you are already forgiven. And to be forgiven means you are set free from the shame of your sexual sin.

It is the responsibility of the church to surround those who have been blistered and burned by their sexual choices. The church was never meant to be a pristine showroom. It was meant to be a messy living room filled with people who have messed up. So we have a faucet that we never turn off, and what flows out isn't finger pointing and rock throwing. What flows out of the church is what flows out of Jesus—help, hope, and healing.

If the gospel is for *everyone*, then the church is for *everyone* too.

Heather was raped when she was a sophomore in college. When she learned she was pregnant, she chose to have an abortion. At the time, she couldn't imagine raising a child fathered by such a terrible man. Her family members pressured her into doing it early in the pregnancy because they told her the emotional fallout would be less significant. But in the years that followed, that wasn't the case.

Heather felt dirty. She felt stained by her choice.

That's shame.

Years of counseling and a loving group of friends have helped her process the difficult decision she made years ago. Twenty years later she is finally experiencing the freedom that flows from forgiveness.

"For a student to go on a field trip to the zoo, that student needs a parent's signature. But that same student can terminate a pregnancy without parental endorsement," she told me recently. "You can go to jail for two years if you destroy an eagle's egg. So what's inside an eagle's egg is more valuable than what is inside a woman's stomach? Someone needs to say something about this so no one else experiences what I've experienced."

I didn't know what to say.

But if you are a young woman and you come to me and say, "Jon, I'm pregnant and I'm scared, and I don't want the rest of my life to be ruined by one mistake, so I'm thinking about getting an abortion," I now know what to say.

"Please don't do it. You may have an unwanted pregnancy, but you don't have an unwanted baby."

Every year more than one million babies are aborted in this country, while every year between one and two million couples in this country put their names on a waiting list to adopt a child. There are more parents than there are babies.

Outspoken atheist Richard Dawkins responded to a question on Twitter about what a woman who is pregnant with a child with Down syndrome should do. His advice?

"Abort it and try again. It would be immoral to bring it into the world if you have the choice," he tweeted back.

I read about a church where all nine hundred members volunteered to adopt a little boy with Down syndrome whose mom was contemplating aborting him.

May we be as proactive as we are reactive to this issue. May we be the kind of people who will care for any kind of children born into this world.

If we love Jesus, we will love both the woman and the baby she is carrying.

To all the women who have had an abortion, and to all the men who pushed them to do so, I believe there is hope for you. I want you to know that Satan cannot steal your salvation. But he can steal the joy of your salvation.

Satan likes to take the stain of our sin and rub it in deep. He wants to chain you to your past, lock you up in a prison of spiritual and emotional limbo, and throw away the key. But Jesus wants you to be set free from the weight of your secret and from the embarrassment of your shame.

One woman I know wrote, "Twenty years ago I had an abortion. In that moment I had to put my heart in the deep freeze in order to not be bothered by the act. But my heart has been thawing out for the last few years and as it gets warmer and more tender, I feel more alive."

I want that for you.

Telling someone, "I had an abortion," isn't the only step to healing, but it is the first step: "Confess your sins to each other and pray for each other so that you may be healed" (James 5:16 NIV).

As awkward as it may feel to raise the blinds on the dark part of your past, do it. Let the light of God's love drive out your pain. And do it for others.

My sister Julie has eight children. Her last two children are boys—Jon and Jack.

ME TOO

Several years ago, before Allison and I had children, we babysat for them and were giving five of them a bath at once. It was complete pandemonium. Naked kids running everywhere!

In the midst of the bubbles, we lost Jon and Jack. I couldn't find them anywhere. Then I heard the sound of giggling coming from my sister's bedroom, so I opened the door. On the other side of the bed, hidden from view, Jon and Jack were lying on the floor naked, laughing like two old men.

It made me laugh too!

They had taken a huge container of baby powder, had emptied it on each other, and were rubbing it in.

When they saw me, one of them said, "This is what our dad does after a shower." And the other one said, "You oughta try it, Uncle Jon! It feels awesome!"

A few years ago, my sister was in the basement picking up toys and doing laundry when it got really quiet upstairs—always a sign that her little ones are up to no good. So when she went upstairs and turned the corner, she discovered that someone had taken a red marker and an orange marker and had drawn a squiggly line on the wall. It went from one end of the hallway to the other.

She called for Jon and Jack, but no answer. So she just followed the line, and it ended at a closet in one of the bedrooms. She slowly opened the closet door and there they stood. She said she tried not to laugh, but Jon was covered from head to toe in red marker and Jack was covered from head to toe in orange marker. She looked at both of them and said, "Do either of you know who colored my walls?"

At the same time, with orange and red marker all over their faces, Jon shook his head no and Jack nodded his head yes.

I think the technical term for it is "Busted!"

Thirteen years ago my sister went into the hospital with a pain in her chest. She was five months pregnant with Jack, so we flew to Missouri to be with her and my brother-in-law. The doctor told my sister that she had a huge blood clot, and that if she didn't abort her baby, she might die.

My sister is one of the sweetest people God put on the planet. But her convictions run deep.

"I'll die," she said, "before I let you take the life of my baby."

If my sister had listened to that doctor, I wouldn't have a nephew named Jack who is an absolute blessing and joy in my life.

Like suicide, abortion is a subject that I believe we have to have a better response for. It's an opportunity to love people the way we've been loved. Totally. Unconditionally. Loved.

Abortion can end with this generation. If we are going to be responsible enough to have sex, then we need to be responsible enough to raise the children that sex produces. So to everyone who calls themselves a follower of Jesus, let's be unified in our message—adoption is the best option.

We don't bomb clinics. We don't kill doctors. We don't condemn scared women. Instead, we do what God did for us. We adopt children into our families.

Proverbs 31:8 says, "Open your mouth for the speechless."

On behalf of the next sixty million babies who don't have a voice, let's throw lavish baby showers for unwed moms. Let's pick them up and sit with them at their medical appointments. Let's volunteer to rock their babies in the middle of the night. Let's financially support the work of our local crisis pregnancy centers. Let's do whatever we can do to be considerate of all life—the life of the baby and the life of the mom, so that the life of the church has a future.

And above all else, may this next generation be more effective than my generation and any previous generation at proclaiming the message of the angels when they declared to the world two thousand years ago: "Do not be afraid. I bring you good news that will cause great joy for all the people. Today in the town of David a Savior has been born to you; he is the Messiah, the Lord" (Luke 2:10–11 NIV).

He is Jesus. The source of our help. The source of our hope. The source of our healing.

HOSPITALITY: WELCOME MATS AND BLACK MAGIC MARKERS

I TOOK MY FAMILY TO AN INDOOR GO-KART TRACK IN LEXINGTON. WE WENT later in the evening to avoid the crowds, but when we walked in, we were surprised to see a group of about thirty Muslim women standing in line. They were wearing their traditional long dresses and head coverings. Apart from the teenagers who worked there, they were the only people in the massive warehouse.

I can either show them the love of Jesus or run them off the track! I thought to myself.

I looked at my son as he rubbed his hands together. He had a mischievous smile on his face. "This is going to be fun!" he said.

I knew he wasn't thinking about Jesus. He was thinking about jihad. Go-kart holy war is what he wanted to start!

Jesus seemed to live with a welcome mat at his feet. With the exception of legalistic religious leaders, everyone felt safe entering Jesus' personal space. I want to carry myself in such a way that people feel welcomed around me.

We built our house with hospitality in mind. Allison loves to cook, so we have two tables inside our house and two tables outside our house for people to put their feet under. We love watching people move from outside our home to inside our home. There is something about getting people in our homes that keeps them in our hearts.

Last summer I went to visit my friend Bob. He invited a bunch of friends to his house in Canada. I've never been around anyone who understands hospitality better than Bob and Maria Goff and their two sons. Every minute of every day was filled with food and fun. I've never laughed or cried as much in three days as I did with Bob and his family.

Bob and Maria have this really cool practice that we've adopted at our house. Everyone who eats at their table is invited to sign the bottom of the table before they leave. There isn't a square inch of space under their table that isn't covered in names.

Jesus told us to make disciples. That's our job description—to make more and better disciples. But disciples aren't made overnight. It's people intensive and time intensive. And it requires hospitality.

The old saying, "People don't care how much you know until they know how much you care," is equal parts cheesy and true.

When you place a welcome mat at the entrance of your heart, Jesus moves in and expands your capacity to care for other people. He adds square footage by renovating and ripping out any tendency in us to compete against people. Then he furnishes it with a desire to celebrate people. There is enough competition in our world, but there isn't enough celebration.

Most people in our culture have been wounded by someone in their families, which leads me to believe that most healing that needs to take place in their lives needs to take place in the context of a caring family.

Psalm 68:6 says, "God sets the solitary in families."

So often when we build our homes, we think of comfort first. What if when we built our homes we thought of compassion first? What if our compassion was greater than our comfort?

What if we set a place at our tables for the lonely? What if our homes became safe places for people who have been bruised and battered by their families? What if people walked into our homes with hurt, but left with healing?

I want every square inch of wood on our dining room table to be covered in names. It's so fun handing a black magic marker to our guests and watching them slide under the table to put their John Hancock on it.

Years ago I was sitting in a car with a friend at a busy intersection here in Lexington when two boys crossed the street in front of us. Both of them looked to be in their early teenage years. One could walk without assistance, while the other one had braces on both legs.

The one with the braces struggled to get across the street. Every step required great effort and concentration.

On the other side of the street was a retaining wall. The healthy boy jumped on top of it with ease, but the boy with braces on his legs didn't even try. Instead, he turned around, backed up to the wall, and raised his arms in the air. I watched as the boy on top of the wall bent over and lifted his friend to where he was.

I realize there are people who don't want to be helped. But most who need help, want help. So what if we spent our lives pulling people up to where we are?

I hit the parent lottery when I was born. I grew up in a healthy, loving home with parents who invited people from all walks of life to put their feet under our dining room table. My parents showed me how to pick people up who had been knocked down in life—from hitchhikers to addicts to ex-cons to the mentally and physically challenged.

My parents had the capacity to care. They had a huge welcome mat at the entrance of their hearts and their home. Their compassion was greater than their comfort.

Years ago, at the church where I serve, we realized people were spending too much time in our buildings and on our campuses.

We realized too many people were coming to church while not enough people were being the church.

Some people were spiritually overeating, getting fat on biblical facts, but never sharing the nourishment with others who were starving for hope. As leaders, we knew we needed to put some folks on a diet. So we unplugged a ton of programs and challenged people to take what they knew about God and apply it to people who knew nothing about him.

We passed out welcome mats and black markers. As a result, our church grew numerically and spiritually.

As in our homes, the churches we are a part of can become places of comfort. Pews can turn into La-Z-Boys. Sermons can turn into shows. Worship can turn into entertainment. But everything changes in a church when you are sitting next to someone whose eternity hangs in the balance.

Every so often I challenge our church family by saying, "If you never bring a nonbeliever to church with you, you will never understand anything we do as a church. But the minute you bring a nonbeliever to church with you, you will understand everything we do as a church."

There are enough churches that shut their doors on sinners like me. We want people to know that the more sinful they are, the more welcome they will be at our church.

I think that's why I love fireflies.

ME TOO

We have a field near our house, and I was outside the other night with my kids. Against the backdrop of a dark sky, it was as if the field was glowing.

Jesus said, "You are the light of the world. A city that is set on a hill cannot be hidden. Nor do they light a lamp and put it under a basket, but on a lampstand, and it gives light to all who are in the house. Let your light so shine before men, that they may see your good works and glorify your Father in heaven" (Matt. 5:14–16).

Fireflies don't light up in a coordinated way. They light up at different times and in different places, but there is no denying their light-giving ability. They stand out in the darkness.

And that's how the church is supposed to function. When someone cooks a meal for a family in need, fills someone's car with gas, or mows the yard of a widow, the world turns its head and takes notice. Flashes of light grab our attention.

You don't have to be the biggest light or the brightest light to make a difference in someone's life. You just have to be the closest. Love the person closest to you.

I had the privilege of baptizing a man who was invited to our church by a friend of his. They hadn't seen each other in over twenty years, but at a high school reunion earlier in the year, they had reconnected. As they were hanging out at a local restaurant catching up on lost time, both of them laughed about how out of shape they had gotten since their days of playing football in high school.

"Hey, I've always wanted to run in the Bluegrass 10,000," one of them said. "Why don't we train together?"

So every evening after work, they met at a local park and ran together. Or as one of them said, "We limped fast!"

Over a three-week period of running in circles, huffing and puffing and gasping for air, they learned that over the past two decades both of them had gone through ugly divorces, lost their jobs at one point, and lost a parent to cancer.

The one thing they didn't have in common was church. One had a church family to help him get through it, and the other one didn't.

I heard a preacher say, "You can either put a cross or a scarecrow at the front door of your church. One makes people want to come in, and the other makes them want to leave."

Live with a welcome mat at your feet and a black marker in your hand. God will give people directions to your house.

13

AVAILABILITY: TRAPPED ON A PLANE WITH A SKUNK

WHEN MY DAUGHTER WAS FIVE, I WATCHED HER DANCE IN HER BEDROOM without her knowing I was watching. She curtsied to an unseen, imaginary friend, who I'm guessing was the prince from Cinderella. But she danced around with him and was totally lost in the moment. She whispered and sang and moved around the room until she saw me, and the moment she did, she snapped out of her imagination—leaving whatever reality she was in to come back to this one. But I could tell that wherever she was and whomever she was with, it was very real to her.

When my son was three, he had two imaginary horses that he kept tied up to the kitchen table. One was named Spirit and the other was named Melissa. I'm pretty sure Melissa was named after a girl in his preschool who drove him crazy!

But better than his two horses was his imaginary brother named Sea Cai. For two years Silas talked about his sixteen-year-old brother named Sea Cai. If I asked Silas to brush his teeth or eat his green beans, he would say, "Well, my sixteen-year-old brother Sea Cai doesn't have to, so I don't have to either."

Somewhere out there I have a defiant and illegitimate son of Eskimo descent!

After two years of hearing about this sixteen-year-old brother none of us could see, Ava came into our bedroom one night. She said, "Dad, I don't think Silas has a brother. I don't think Sea Cai is real at all!"

It took her two years to figure it out, but by golly she got to the bottom of it!

For many people, God is nothing more than a childish fantasy, a figment of the human imagination, or a fictional character in a fairy tale. The only problem with that line of thinking is the person known in history as Jesus of Nazareth. Because the stakes are so high, every person on the planet has to wrestle with the life of Jesus. Was he just a man, or was he who he claimed to be—God in human skin?

I've always believed that if you can believe the first sentence of the Bible, you won't have any trouble believing any other sentence in the Bible. But the first sentence is a doozy! "In the beginning God created the heavens and the earth" (Gen. 1:1).

Out of nothing he made everything. And if he made you, he can heal you. More important than his ability to heal you is his desire to heal you.

He wants to.

He does not want your past to affect your future. Rough childhood, ugly divorce, suffocating addiction, unbearable loneliness or insecurity about the way you look—whatever contagious issue you carry from day to day that has affected and infected every area of your life—Jesus wants to take that from you.

We see this reality in Jesus' interaction with a leper. "A man with leprosy came and knelt in front of Jesus, begging to be healed. 'If you are willing, you can heal me and make me clean,' he said.

"Moved with compassion, Jesus reached out and touched him. 'I am willing,' he said. 'Be healed!' Instantly the leprosy disappeared, and the man was healed" (Mark 1:40–42 NLT).

Leprosy is a word that means "to peel off." It was used to describe several different skin diseases in that time period, but it always resulted in death. What scared most people was the contagious nature of the disease. People suffering from leprosy were removed from their homes and forced to live a life of banishment on the outskirts of society.

In order to be able to identify who had leprosy and who didn't, lepers were forced to wear bells around their necks, grow their hair out, and yell, "Unclean! Unclean!" when approaching a person or a crowd. "If someone can heal a leper," Jewish rabbis would say, "they are also capable of raising the dead."

Death and leprosy were synonymous. A person could be alive, but they were treated as if they were already dead.

Cholera outbreaks were not uncommon in this country in the 1800s. To keep the disease from spreading, grave diggers would bury people as quickly as possible upon death. But many people feared they were burying people who weren't dead yet.

To appease people who had this fear, city officials ordered morticians to tie a string around the buried person's finger that led to a bell aboveground. If they happened to "wake up," they could ring the bell. There are stories of "dead" people who rang the bells.

For many people, life has become a coffin or a prison cell where they feel trapped. They don't see a way out of the situation they find themselves in.

In the movie *The Shawshank Redemption*, one of the characters is a man named Red who was imprisoned for the majority of his adult life. He becomes so institutionalized he can't imagine life as a free man. "These walls are funny. First you hate 'em. Then you get used to 'em," he says in one scene. "Enough time passes and you get so you depend on 'em."[1]

Jesus shows up and gives everyone the opportunity to ring

the bell. Jesus provides the opportunity to escape death and experience the freedom of life outside the walls.

What I've learned about Jesus is that his life is more contagious than my sickness. The leper's sickness didn't spread to Jesus. Rather, Jesus' life spread to the leper.

Jesus isn't approaching you wearing a surgical mask and rubber gloves. He's never worn a hazmat suit in his life. Your struggle with pornography, your battle with eating disorders, your foul mouth and corrupt heart don't scare him in the least. If you want to be free, he wants to set you free from whatever has banished you to the outskirts of his community and love.

Jesus told the leper he healed not to tell anyone what he'd done for him. "But the man went and spread the word, proclaiming to everyone what had happened. As a result, large crowds soon surrounded Jesus, and he couldn't publicly enter a town anywhere. He had to stay out in the secluded places, but people from everywhere kept coming to him" (Mark 1:45 NLT).

By freeing a secluded man, Jesus was forced into seclusion.

In other words, Jesus always gives more than he gets. And what he's given all of us is a second chance at life. Who doesn't want that? Wouldn't it make sense to take the new lease on life we've been given and share it with others the way the leper did?

The leper was commanded to be silent, but he told everyone. We've been commanded to tell everyone, but we remain silent.

And don't misunderstand that statement. I'm not talking about evangelism. I'm not talking about inviting your friends to church or sharing your faith with a family member. I'm talking about a life that is so soaked and saturated with joy and freedom that it stands out in a world of sadness and death.

I have a friend named Morris who is battling Parkinson's disease and Alzheimer's. It's a bad combination for a good man.

Every day Morris sits on his front porch and watches birds, people walking their dogs, and the cars that drive by. I wave to him every time we drive to the baseball field where my son plays.

What I love about Morris is that he prays while he sits there. Even though his mind isn't as sharp as it once was, he asks God to give him opportunities to share his faith with people.

One day a seven-year-old neighbor came up on the porch and asked Morris if he wanted to play army with him. "I was once in the army," Morris told him, a big smile on his face. "But I'm not as mobile as I used to be, so I'll have to play while sitting in this chair."

The boy thought that was a great idea, so he and Morris re-enacted several famous war scenes.

Morris, like me, is married to someone he doesn't deserve. His wife, June, walks with God.

"We need to invite that boy to church," Morris whispered to June one afternoon. "God wants us to do that."

ME TOO

June didn't know if Morris was thinking clearly, but she knew Morris's heart was in the right place. So she walked across the street and invited the boy and his mom to visit our church.

"I haven't been to church in over twenty years, and my son has never been," the woman said. "We'd love to come!"

There is a family in our church that has adopted several children from several different countries. Most of the children they've adopted have special needs. They recently adopted a little boy from China who has Down syndrome. I had the privilege of filling out some of the paperwork for him, so when he finally made it to the United States, I couldn't wait to meet him.

His name is Isaac, and he let me pick him up. When I did, he hugged me and nestled his head into my chest just under my chin. I walked around the room for a few minutes thanking God for him and his new family.

Then he said, "I need to pee!" He's learning English quickly.

I'm learning a lot about freedom from people who seem trapped.

The average flower shop in our city throws away thirty flowers a day. Since there are forty flower shops in town, that is twelve hundred flowers a day that are going to waste—flowers that could have been delivered to someone with a life-giving message attached.

AVAILABILITY: TRAPPED ON A PLANE WITH A SKUNK

I've noticed drugstores popping up on every corner. More and more people are in need of medicine to help them sleep, overcome sadness, and deal with anxiety. I would love for us to give out the same number of flowers as we do pills.

Instead of letting someone sit at home alone in a quiet house thinking about how horrible life is, they could sit at a dining room table while reading a card with some kind words, staring at a vase of flowers that says, "We think you're a beautiful person!"

When was the last time you decided you were going to *give* life to others without needing to *get* anything in return? It's such a great way to live!

When was the last time you told your spouse that you are more committed to them today than you were on the day you put a ring on their finger?

When was the last time you told your children that if you had your pick of a hundred kids, you'd pick them every time?

Years ago, a skunk burrowed under our house and gave birth to six baby skunks. Every night they would release their scent under our house, and it would make its way inside. It was such a strong smell that it would wake us up. And we couldn't open the windows and doors to air our house out because the smell outside was worse than the smell inside. We were literally trapped!

ME TOO

I would empty an entire can of Febreze every night, trying to make our sleeping conditions more tolerable.

One morning I took a flight that was bound for Atlanta. About ten minutes into the flight I opened my backpack, which was situated at my feet, and the second I opened it, the smell of skunk wafted up and hit me in the face. It was as if a baby skunk had taken up residence in my backpack!

"That's weird," the businesswoman seated next to me said. "We're thirty thousand feet in the air and I smell a skunk. Do you smell a skunk?"

I laughed and pointed to the guy sitting behind us.

In a matter of seconds our entire section was complaining to the flight attendants about the smell. I know it's not leprosy, but by the end of the flight no one was sitting within five rows of me.

God loves us as we are, but he refuses to leave us as we are.

He has cleaned us up and wants to continue the process. And we will only experience that continued healing from what the world has taken from us and done to us if we stay close to Jesus.

We want to be healed, and he wants to heal us.

It's what we do once we're healed that will tell whether we really appreciate what Jesus has done for us.

14

UNITY: GOOD DONUTS, BAD THEOLOGY

ONE OF MY WEAKNESSES IS MY APPETITE FOR DONUTS. ONE OF MY strengths is my appetite for donuts.

Every Saturday morning in college a group of guys from the dorm I lived in would pile into a car and head to a local donut store that epitomized the word *dive*. The outside of the building was in desperate need of a face-lift, and the inside wasn't much better. It was a bare-bones operation, but what they lacked in environment, the owners made up for in taste.

It was a family-run business. The matriarch of the family took the orders while the patriarch of the family, his sons, and their wives rolled out, baked, and dipped the little pieces of glazed heaven. They ran a tight ship, but they were a few burritos shy of a fiesta.

Adorning every square inch of space on the walls were posters of various sizes. Scattered on the tables and front counter were brochures that I never bothered to read. But one time, during what would be my final trip into the store, I decided to read a few of them.

One of the brochures talked about burning down abortion clinics. Another talked about creating an island to put gay people on. The last one I read was so racist in its tone that I couldn't finish reading it. Each brochure distorted scripture to back up its message.

I lost my appetite for more than the donuts they were selling.

As I sat there holding their propaganda, that's when it happened.

"Are you boys from the Bible college?" the owner asked, sounding like an angry drill sergeant when he talked.

"Yes, sir. We are," one of my buddies responded politely.

"That's a shame," the owner said. "Clean-cut boys like you, wasting your time with all those false teachers. God knows we need preachers, but not those kind."

I am not a confrontational person, so it took every ounce of courage I could muster to ask him a question. "I mean no disrespect, but how do you read the same Bible we read and justify the messages in your brochures?" I asked.

His response didn't surprise me, but it did sadden me.

"We reserve the right to refuse service to anyone," he said back.

Well, that didn't really answer my question. So I rephrased it.

"You use scripture to justify the killing of people that Jesus died for, and I'm wondering if you could explain that to me?" I asked calmly and quietly.

"Are you hard of hearing?" he asked. "We reserve the right to refuse service to anyone!" Every word came out of his mouth slowly and loudly, as if he thought I was hard of hearing and unable to speak English. We left and never went back.

Followers of Jesus who hate people? I didn't know it was possible because it isn't possible. Love unites people. Legalism divides people. "Legalism has no pity on people," said Max Lucado. "Legalism makes my opinion your burden, makes my opinion your boundary, makes my opinion your obligation."[1]

Legalism is a knee-jerk response to liberal theology. When a culture establishes its own moral code to live by, the tendency is for people who love God to lose sight of grace and demand an exact obedience to a different moral code.

During the time of Jesus, the Pharisees were devoted to God and his law, and they were the walking, talking, eating, sleeping, breathing definition of what it means to be legalistic. And Jesus

131

tried to steer them toward a relationship with God instead of a religion for God.

God designed a day of rest called the Sabbath. *Sabbath* is a word that means "stop." God wants his people to have a day where they stop working and start resting. But the Pharisees twisted it and complicated it. They took something good and made it bad.

They wouldn't have allowed you to dip a radish in salt on the Sabbath day because it would cause the radish to pickle, and if the radish pickled, then you would be guilty of causing the radish to work.

You couldn't throw an object in the air and catch it with the other hand because the Pharisees considered that to be work, but you *could* throw an object in the air and catch it with the same hand you threw it with.

The Pharisees would have hated baseball.

In Matthew 23, Jesus leveled some harsh accusations against the Pharisees—accusations that would lead them to crucify him. Jesus accused them of evangelizing people into hell, oppressing people through religious rituals, having a purity that was only external, and killing the prophets.

Strong words from a strong leader who wanted his followers to be united around the mission of love, not divided over a list of rules.

In high school I had a friend named Maddie. When she was fifteen years old, she became pregnant after having sex for the first time. Her family was able to keep the pregnancy a secret for a few months, but when Maddie started to show, word quickly spread through our church.

I can still see Maddie's family walking down the side aisle, her head bowed in shame as she sat between her nervous parents. I can still see people staring at her as if she were carrying a deadly virus. And I can still hear the low-grade whisper that filled the awkward silence of the sanctuary—a sanctuary where hundreds of sermons on grace had been preached, where hundreds of lives had been saved.

But no one spoke to Maddie. Instead, everyone spoke about Maddie. People who get grace from God don't always give grace to others.

In my lifetime, I've watched churches split over whether or not women should wear pants or whether or not drums should be played in worship. I've received e-mails asking if I thought it was okay to cover stained-glass windows with tinted windows. I've been stopped in public and told I was in violation of scripture because the church where I serve uses crackers for Communion instead of unleavened bread.

"A church without a pulpit is a church without God," one old man told me. We were standing in line at a grocery store when he decided to give me a lecture on stage furniture.

"I'm glad Jesus had twelve friends to help him carry his wooden pulpit around Galilee," I said with a smile on my face. I paid for my milk, patted him on the back, and prayed for him as I walked to my car.

Years ago my dad mediated between two groups of people in a church who were upset with one another because the carpet in the lobby needed to be replaced and they disagreed about what color to choose.

Is it any wonder why so many people like my friend Maddie want nothing to do with Jesus and his followers?

"I like your Christ. I do not like your Christians," Gandhi once said. "Your Christians are so unlike your Christ."

I approach parenting with a simple mind-set: Love before law. Relationship before rules. Every command God gives us is an invitation into a better life, not a requirement for love. And I want my kids to realize that the purpose of rules isn't to get love from me, but to experience the fullness of love that I have for them.

That's precisely why Jesus prayed for his followers to be unified and not divided. He wants us to experience the fullness of the Father's love for us.

There are people who claim to love God, but they don't love people. If you love God, you will love people, including people you disagree with. Followers of Jesus are not given the luxury of having enemies.

Legalism creates enemies, not friends. Love creates friends, not enemies.

Chuck Swindoll wrote:

> There are killers on the loose today. The problem is that you can't tell by looking. They don't wear little buttons that give away their identity, nor do they carry signs warning everybody to stay away. On the contrary, a lot of them carry Bibles and appear to be clean-living, nice-looking, law-abiding citizens. Most of them spend a lot of time in churches, some in places of religious leadership. Many are so respected in the community, their neighbors would never guess they are living next door to killers.
>
> They kill freedom, spontaneity, and creativity; they kill joy as well as productivity. They kill with their words and their pens and their looks. They kill with their attitudes far more often than with their behavior. There is hardly a church or Christian organization or Christian school or missionary group or media ministry where such danger does not lurk. The amazing thing is that they get away with it, day in and day out, without being confronted or exposed. Strangely, the same ministries that would not tolerate heresy for ten minutes will step aside and allow these killers all the space they need to maneuver and manipulate others in the most insidious manner imaginable. Their intolerance is tolerated. Their judgmental spirits remain unjudged. Their bullying tactics

continue unchecked. And their narrow-mindedness is either explained away or quickly defended. The bondage that results would be criminal were it not so subtle and wrapped in such spiritual-sounding garb.

This day—this very moment—millions who should be free, productive individuals are living in shame, fear, and intimidation. They are victimized, existing as if they were living on death row instead of enjoying the beauty and fresh air of the abundant life Christ modeled and made possible for all of His followers to claim.[2]

The church needs less legalism and more love. We need to rally around what we agree about, not what we disagree about. Jesus didn't die so his people would fight over the color of carpet in the lobby. He died so people could become sons and daughters of God.

Think about all the people Jesus healed—the leper, the blind man, the dead girl, the paralytic, the demon-possessed man. Now think about what would have happened to those people if Jesus had said, "I can't heal you until you do this . . ." Jesus healed them before he expected anything from them.

"Go and sin no more," was a phrase he said *after* healing people, not before.

Twenty-five years ago, a pastor in our city asked a young woman to leave the church he was leading because of her sin. She wasn't a Christian. She was investigating Christ, but this man who claimed to be a Christian caused her to not visit another church for more than two decades.

Time passed and so did the pastor. At the invitation of a friend she decided to give Christ and Christians another chance.

I was preaching about the woman caught in adultery the weekend she visited. As a way of making the message memorable, we had huge piles of rocks at each of our entrances, and each person was encouraged to pick up a rock before the service began. Instead of challenging our church not to judge people, I challenged them to forgive the people who had judged them. As we sang the last song, a line of people walked up and tearfully let go of the hurt, pain, and anger they were holding on to as a result of other people being mean to them. Everyone let go of a rock that day, with the exception of our visitor who had been judged twenty-five years earlier.

She had been condemned by so many Christians so many times in her life that her grip on the rock didn't loosen. It tightened.

For three months, she engaged in an anonymous e-mail correspondence with me. During each exchange I learned something new about her past. As time went by, she seemed to realize the rock was holding her back and weighing her down.

One evening my phone beeped, indicating I had received a new e-mail. It was an invitation to baptize someone, but the person didn't want to reveal who they were. So I showed up the next evening in my swimming trunks and shook hands with a middle-aged woman. Unbeknownst to me, it was the woman I had been corresponding with.

A woman who had been asked in the past to leave the church was now coming to the church to leave her past behind.

As we stepped down into the water, she set a rock on the lip of the baptism pool, and it finally hit me who she was. I started to cry and she started to cry, and I know God smiled.

"I'm done holding on to the rocks that people have thrown at me, and I'm ready to take hold of the hand of Jesus instead," she said with confidence.

"The church didn't die for you. That pastor who asked you to leave didn't die for you," I told her. "Jesus died for you." In that beautiful moment, love triumphed over the law.

15

SPONTANEITY: A BOAT IN COMMERCE, OKLAHOMA

LAST SUMMER SILAS AND I COMPLETED A HIGH ROPES COURSE IN THE Appalachian Mountains. We were partnered with a couple we didn't know, so before the instructor explained the activities of the day, I introduced myself to them. If I was going to spend four hours dangling from a rope sixty feet above the ground with them, getting to know them seemed the right thing to do. The odd thing about the introduction was the obvious age difference between the man and the woman.

He was in his mid- to late fifties, and she was in her mid- to late teens.

"How are you all related?" was how I chose to break the ice.

"Oh, we're married," he said quickly and defensively.

I was hoping you wouldn't say that, I thought to myself, not saying it out loud.

There were a few moments of awkward silence, so I decided to follow it up with a second question. "How did you meet?" I asked.

"We met while playing video games online," he said. "She's from France and I'm from Canada."

Before I could stop him, my son launched a social grenade by saying, "That's really weird! I thought only kids played video games!"

I quickly put my hand over his mouth and said, "That's not weird! We're all weird! I'm weird! My son is weird! Spending a day wearing a helmet and a harness is weird!"

No amount of damage control could repair the lingering tension Silas created in that moment. As we climbed up to the first platform, he added to it by saying to the guy, "I thought she was your daughter!"

If I could've gotten my money back, I would have quit before we started. The next four hours were some of the longest of my life! Fortunately for us, the girl didn't speak English, so she didn't understand anything that had been said.

On every level, my son is a risk taker and not a play-it-safer kind of kid. *Caution* is a cuss word to Silas. He loves adventure, and I love him for that.

One of his best friends is a boy named Matthew. Matthew lives on a farm and has the best southern accent of anyone I know. He and Silas spend hours riding dirt bikes, digging holes, and shooting things with their BB guns.

When Matthew spent the night with us recently, he told our family over dinner that one of his cows had been bitten by a copperhead, a highly venomous snake.

"Yep, her head and leg swelled up so big we hardly recognized her," he said with a country twang that rivaled Reba McEntire's.

As startled and saddened as we were by the details of his story, it's what he said next that shocked us.

"We finally took her out back and shot her behind her ear," he said nonchalantly. "Sometimes you just have to shoot 'em, Mr. Weece . . . you just have to shoot 'em."

Trying not to laugh, I took a huge bite out of a dinner roll and said, "You're so right, Matthew. Sometimes, you just have to shoot 'em."

Jesus had friends like Silas and Matthew. He surrounded himself with guys who weren't afraid to say or do anything. One of them was named Peter.

As Jesus walked across the surface of a lake, Peter said, "Lord, if it is You, command me to come to You on the water" (Matt. 14:28).

Peter was a risk taker and not a play-it-safer kind of guy.

"Come," Jesus said (Matt. 14:29).

With one word, Jesus dared Peter to do something no one else had ever done.

Do you have friends who dare you to take risks or friends who expect you to play it safe? Do you have friends who dare you to spend your vacation time in Africa serving at an orphanage? Do you have friends who dare you to give away more money this year than you did last year? Do you have friends who dare you to memorize a chapter of the Bible, change careers, lose weight, or seek counseling?

Jesus was the kind of friend who dared his friends to grow their faith by facing their fears.

At the heart of a "me too" community is a desire to push the boundaries of what's possible. "Me too" people never settle for the status quo. They have more faith than fear because they take more risks than most people.

"Whatever scares you the most is what you need to do," one of my friends said to another friend.

At lunch one day, my buddy was talking about a new job opportunity in Colorado. Another friend with us dared him to do whatever would increase his trust in God. I will never forget that conversation or that advice.

Peter doesn't ask for comfort. Peter asks for a command.

And once Jesus commanded him to get out of the boat, Peter didn't hesitate or make excuses. Peter got out of the boat! I'm sure in that moment his knees were knocking and his hands were shaking. I'm sure his buddies were trying to convince him that he shouldn't do it.

"It's too risky, Peter!" they probably shouted. "You have a wife and kids to think of!"

You find out how strong your faith is when you step out to a place where your faith can be tested. Staying in the boat doesn't keep you safe. It just keeps you the same.

The community Jesus created with his twelve closest friends was a community that avoided comfort at all costs. They looked for ways to obey the commands of God, putting God's power to the test by putting themselves in positions where they couldn't determine or manipulate the outcome. So it's no wonder they changed the world!

Peter wasn't a boat potato. He was a wave rider. And yet so many preachers talk about how Peter lacked faith and failed once he stepped out of the boat.

Sure, Peter sank, but he was the only one in the boat who got out in the first place. He didn't lack a quality of faith; he lacked a quantity of faith. And yes, he failed, but he failed within reach of Jesus. And that is the key.

"Immediately Jesus stretched out His hand and caught him" (Matt. 14:31).

You're going to fail, I'm going to fail, we're all going to fail at a variety of things in life, but many people fail far from the hand of Jesus. That is tragic, because Jesus is the only friend strong enough to lift us out of our failures.

Notice, Jesus didn't laugh at Peter when his fear kicked into overdrive. Jesus didn't hold Peter's head under the water and say, "Serves you right!"

No, Jesus will never shame you when you fail, which is why all of us need friends who encourage us to get closer to Jesus.

Jesus saved Peter from drowning, then walked with him back to the boat. With Jesus helping him, Peter did what no one else in the boat did—nor anyone else in history for that matter—and that is walk on water.

Peter walked on water!

We all need friends who encourage us to do what we enjoy. So many followers of Jesus look and act as if they have a stomachache. They need to drink some Pepto-Bismol, figure out what they love, and do more of it.

When people get burned out in their careers, I encourage them to choose satisfaction over salary. God made all of us *on* purpose and *for* a purpose, so we shouldn't apologize for choosing to spend our lives doing the things we love.

"Do what you enjoy, and you'll enjoy what you do," is what my dad used to say to me when I was trying to figure out how to honor God with my life.

I love to help people, so that's how I spend my time.

I've mentioned that my wife, Allison, loves to cook, and so does her good friend Kelly. So once a week they cook a few meals for families with busy schedules and bless them with food. People love to eat what Allison and Kelly cook because they're both great cooks.

So do what you enjoy doing, and do what you're good at.

I cringe every time I watch *American Idol* because every season there is a handful of people who enjoy singing, but no one enjoys hearing them. All of us need friends who encourage us to do what we're good at and discourage us from doing what we're not good at.

One of my favorite professors in college was also one of the most practical professors I had in college. "Let someone's misery become your ministry," he would say with passion.

As I said, I love to help people, and there are people who need to be helped, so that has become my ministry. Every person needs to look at the world, and if there is something in the world that bothers them, they should spend their lives eliminating that need.

Remember Popeye the Sailor Man? He was tired of getting beat up, and every episode he would say, "That's all I can stands, I can't stands it no more!" Every person on the planet needs to have one of those moments when they look at the world we live in.

There are people who don't use their turn signals in traffic, and there are men who wear capri pants. Both things bother me, but I'm not going to spend my life trying to help those people figure it out. But I will help engineers figure out ways to dig wells where safe drinking water isn't accessible to millions of people. I will help doctors figure out ways to get vaccinations to villages where the infant mortality rate is ridiculously high. I will help teachers figure out ways to teach people how to read so they can read the Bible in their own languages.

There are a lot of things about our world that bother me, and I can help eliminate those things. But staying in the boat and playing it safe isn't going to eliminate anything.

As Mother Teresa was cleaning out a leper's sore, a journalist who was shadowing her for a day said, "I wouldn't do that for a million bucks!"

"Neither would I," was Mother Teresa's response.

There are four million people in the state I live in who don't know about the love of Jesus. And it's not because they can't find a church. They just can't find a church that will tell them about the love of Jesus. So that's why I do what I do. I wake up every morning with a passion to put a church in every city in Kentucky—a church that will do everything possible to let everyone know that God loves them and put his Son on a cross to prove it.

What do you see in our world today that makes you say, "Somebody needs to do something about *that*"? That someone is you! Do *that*! Be *that* person!

Whatever scares you the most is probably what you need to do the most because it will require the most faith. And this is what pleases God the most.

Years ago when I was trying to figure out if I should preach, I first needed to figure out if I *could* preach. So the very first church I preached in was in Commerce, Oklahoma, where the men are men and so are some of the women! I'm pretty sure everyone in attendance that Sunday was chewing tobacco and carrying a pistol.

I was so nervous the night before I was supposed to preach that I almost called to cancel. But something in me knew that I needed to seize the opportunity right in front of me—because if we aren't faithful with "what is," we'll never experience "what could be."

I'm glad I preached in Commerce, Oklahoma. I got out of the boat in that city.

ME TOO

In 1994, in the city of Kigali, Rwanda, a tribal leader for the Hutu people was assassinated. Tensions between the Hutu and the Tutsi people had always been high, but this was an event that proved to be the undoing of an entire nation.

Following the assassination, Hutu radio broadcasters immediately called for the total extermination of the Tutsi tribe. "Pick up your machetes and cut your enemies to pieces," is what one DJ said.

But another man, a simple man named Paul, decided to do just the opposite. He was the manager of a four-star hotel called the Mille Collines. He was also a Hutu who was married to a Tutsi woman.

As neighbors turned against one another in what would become one of the biggest bloodbaths the world has ever seen, Paul transformed the hotel into a safe haven for women and children.

One million people were murdered over a hundred-day period, but Paul was able to rescue twelve hundred people through a simple act of kindness.

"As the world closed its eyes," he said, "I opened my arms."

He was a risk taker, not a play-it-safer.

May the same be said of us as we create safe places for at-risk people.

PART 3

THE CITY—WHAT JESUS WILL DO

I LOVE TO VISIT CITIES BECAUSE I LIVE IN THE COUNTRY.

I've been to New York, Los Angeles, Chicago, Miami, Dallas, and Seattle. I've even crossed the big oceans to see places such as Vienna and Hong Kong and London and Cairo.

The reason I love to visit cities is because there are more options there. There are more places to eat, more places to shop, more museums to visit, more entertainment to enjoy, and more people to see.

And in every major city in the world, you'll find some great parks. Right in the middle of the cement towers and paved roads are small patches of green grass and tall trees. In the midst of all the taxis honking and people talking is a haven of rest and solitude.

Heaven is a city with a garden in the middle of it. And in the middle of the garden is a river with trees lining either side of it. The trees have leaves on their branches that will bring healing to all who sit in their shade.

More importantly, the Gardener will be there. We know him as Jesus. As we heal from all that the world has done to us and taken from us, Jesus will wipe every tear from every eye.

We won't hear guns going off or sirens blaring or babies crying or people yelling in the city Jesus is building for us. We will take a deep breath in the new city. We will rest in the eternal city.

Unlike the cities I've visited in my life, we can't get to heaven by plane, bus, boat, or train. Jesus is coming to get us so he can take us there.

With your permission, that is what we're going to explore in these next chapters.

16

SENSITIVITY: FLIGHT 5191

FEW THINGS IN LIFE SCARE ME MORE THAN THE EXPIRATION DATE ON A gallon of milk. You can smell it all you want, but you won't know if it's good or not unless you try it.

Some people are afraid of snakes. Some are afraid of spiders. Others are afraid of heights. And some people are afraid of germs.

I find it funny that we keep hand sanitizer pumps at all the entrances of the church where I serve. Nothing says "Welcome to church!" more than a greeter getting a squirt of hand sanitizer after shaking hands with you.

"God loves you, but I think you're carrying a deadly virus!"

All of us are afraid of something. Whether it's running out of money or being alone or getting cancer, all of us have fears.

Most surveys indicate the number one fear in the United States is public speaking. Number two on the list is death. In an episode of *Seinfeld*, Jerry says, "Now, this means to the average person, if you have to go to a funeral, you're better off in the casket than doing the eulogy."

In my line of work I see a lot of death. And over the years I've noticed that no one wants to die. There are two contributing factors to our fear of death, and both of them are questions that no one has answers for.

When am I going to die?

How am I going to die?

Am I going to die today or twenty years from now? And will I die in a car accident or have a heart attack?

All we are certain of is that we will die.

My dad used to take me to nursing homes when I was a kid. Many of the residents were lonely and rarely had visitors, so he would encourage me to hug or shake the hand of every person we met. He wanted me to touch the people because they needed to be touched.

Some of the people were bedridden, while others could walk but were suffering from dementia. They didn't know who they were or where they were. The sights, sounds, and smells helped me understand that death is among us. We can try to isolate it and contain it by locking people in buildings, but we can't escape it.

After every visit to a nursing home, we would get in the car and my dad would say the same thing: "Be kind to the old man you're becoming."

We were created to live. We were not created to die.

Death is the opposite of God. God is life. So as much as we hate death, God hates it even more. When Jesus was at the tomb of his good friend Lazarus, he cried three separate times.

"Jesus wept" (John 11:35).

The Greek word used for *wept* in that sentence is a word that means to shed tears quietly, in a controlled way.

In John 11, verse 33: "He was deeply moved" (NIV). And again, in verse 38: "Jesus (was) once more deeply moved."

The Greek word used to describe crying in that sentence is a word used to describe a storm on the ocean. It literally means "to be stirred up" or "to be agitated."

Jesus cried quietly and loudly.

In August of 2006, a flight out of Lexington crashed, killing forty-nine of the fifty passengers on board. I was invited by our sheriff and mayor to a local hotel where the family members were notified by the coroner that their loved ones hadn't survived. It was the saddest scene I've ever witnessed in person.

One man picked up his chair and threw it against the wall in anger. A woman who lost her daughter passed out and had to be taken out by paramedics on a stretcher. Most people just cried. I was one of them.

Our church lost several members that day, and I lost a few close friends. One of them was Larry Turner. He was a brilliant educator at the University of Kentucky and an incredible husband and dad. Larry's wife is one of the strongest women I've ever known. She loves life because she loves Jesus. On the night of her husband's death, she went to bed alone and wrote a single sentence in her journal.

"I am not going to be a bitter woman."

Though Lois was deeply saddened by the loss of her husband, she didn't let death plant a seed of bitterness in the soil of her heart.

Have you noticed how obsessed our culture is with avoiding death? From insurance policies to sunscreen to bike helmets, we do everything we can to avoid death. And please don't misunderstand me; I think we should be good stewards of the life God breathed into us. But avoiding death isn't living.

"Death is more universal than life," wrote Alan Sachs. "Everyone dies, but not everyone lives."

I've preached at funerals for thirty-year-olds who packed more living in their short lives than some people who are seventy years of age.

"Teach us to number our days and recognize how few they are; help us to spend them as we should" (Ps. 90:12 TLB).

That's a great anthem for life—God, teach us to count our days and teach us to make our days count.

A thirty-three-year-old truck driver by the name of Larry Walters accomplished his dream of flying, even if his aircraft was a bit unconventional. On July 2, 1982, he took an aluminum folding chair and attached forty-five weather balloons to the back of it. Larry belted himself into the chair. He took some soda, a CB radio to report to his friends on the ground what he was seeing, and a BB gun to shoot the balloons when he wanted to descend.[1]

I don't know Larry, but I love him!

Instead of leisurely floating over his southern California neighborhood, Larry's chair, when cut loose from the ground, shot more than two miles into the air and traveled through the approach corridor to the Long Beach International Airport. Larry started frantically firing his BB gun as fast as he could, which caused him to descend faster than he wanted.

When he landed (and it was rough landing), he admitted to local law enforcement and emergency medical personnel that he was scared to death. When asked by a reporter if he would ever try the stunt again, he said, "You couldn't pay me a million dollars to do it again."

When asked why he did it, he gave a response for the ages.

"You can't sit around all your life!"

As crazy as he is, he's right. Life is a gift to be enjoyed, and so often when we wrap ourselves in yellow caution tape, we not only avoid dying, we avoid living.

"Please don't squander one bit of this marvelous life God has given us" (2 Cor. 6:1 MSG).

I don't want to squander my life. I want to live! Everything inside of me wants to punch death in the face.

There is a website where you can enter your age and a few other facts about your health, and it will spit out your date of death. It's called the Death Clock. According to the Death Clock, I'm going to die on August 2, 2047, at the ripe old age of seventy-four.

I introduced our church to the website, and an eighty-seven-year old woman went home and filled out the online questionnaire. After tallying her vitals, the website told her she was already dead!

Can I encourage you to begin with your end in mind? Picture yourself in a hospital bed, and your family and friends are in the room gathered around you. What do you want the mood to be like in that moment? What do you want the focus of the conversation to be?

I spend a lot of time with hospice helping families say good-bye to their loved ones. The mood is either of two extremes—the family lets go with joy or holds on with despair. The reason some families are able to let go of their loved ones is because their loved ones lived well.

If you want to leave well, live well.

Yes, their families are sad to see them leave this life, but they also rejoice because they know what the next life has in store for them.

The worst funerals are the ones where everyone is lying about the person who died because the person didn't live well. If your family is at a funeral home asking the preacher if you are in heaven or not, odds are you aren't. It's impossible to hide a relationship with Jesus. People who love Jesus live well.

And if you live well, you'll die well.

My mother-in-law, Betty, battled cancer for the final three years of her life, and she lived with us off and on during that time. Sometimes she would wake up in the middle of the night disoriented and nauseated from the chemo and radiation treatments. We awoke to the sound of her falling on numerous occasions. And there were other middle-of-the-night episodes when she threw up in parts of the house that she believed to be the bathroom, but weren't.

It was difficult to watch a very bright and sweet woman lose her physical and emotional faculties. When doctors told us her cancer had spread to her spine and brain, we were strangely relieved for her. Though we didn't want to say good-bye, dying seemed like a better option because she was living with so much pain and confusion.

My dad and Betty died within a month of each other. Preaching at their funerals was a weird combination of joy and sadness. Both of them loved Jesus and lived well, but their presence in our lives would be greatly missed, and I knew it.

In the years that followed, my mom said one of the most difficult parts of her new normal is going to bed alone each night. She doesn't feel safe. And, she's sad.

When two people become one person in marriage and one of the two dies, it leaves a huge void. Half of my mom is dead. The other half is trying to live.

"There is a huge hole in my heart," she said. "The edges of that hole were jagged and sharp in the first few months after your dad died. But time has worn them down." The hole is still there and won't go away until she dies and is reunited with my dad.

So in a strange way, she's actually looking forward to dying. She doesn't have a morbid fixation or fascination with dying, but she no longer dreads it either. She isn't neglecting her role as a mom and grandma, but her kids and grandkids all understand that she was a wife before any of us came along.

For my mom, Paul's words have never made more sense: "To live is Christ, and to die is gain" (Phil. 1:21).

17

RELIABILITY: SIMPLEXITY

AS A KID, I WOULD STEP OFF THE SCHOOL BUS AFTER SCHOOL, RUN INSIDE my house to eat a snack, and run right back outside to play basketball in the driveway. That was my daily routine.

Our neighbor was a sixty-year-old woman named Anita. As I pretended to hit another game-winning shot in the NBA Finals, she would stroll out in her bathrobe smoking a Virginia Slim, pick up her newspaper at the end of the driveway, and go back inside. Anita worked the night shift at a local factory, and she woke up around the time I got home from school.

One particular day, Anita bent over to pick up her newspaper. A strong gust of wind lifted the back of her bathrobe, revealing a side of Anita I had never seen before. For the sake of decency, let's just say she was riding bareback that day!

In a flash (no pun intended), my innocence was robbed. As a ten-year-old boy with midwestern values, I didn't know what to do with what I had just seen. So I stood there holding my basketball with my mouth and eyes wide open.

I was traumatized, Anita was mortified, and both of us ran inside.

Anita called my mom to apologize.

That night as my mom tucked me into bed, she asked, "Jon, is there anything about your day that you want to talk about?"

I wanted to say, "I'm going to need therapy for the rest of my life!" But I was still so shocked by what I had seen that I didn't know what to say. I just shook my head really fast.

Do you ever wish you could replace the bad stuff in your memory with good stuff?

Jesus wants us to have faith like a child. That's not easy to do as an adult. Life as an adult is complex. When I was a kid, life was simple. There is a constant tension in my mind between complexity and simplicity.

I call it simplexity.

I sometimes wish I could live with one eye open and one eye

closed. With the open eye I could see the complexity of our adult world, and with the closed eye I could see the simplicity of my childhood. One eye on earth, one eye on heaven. Nearsighted and farsighted.

Ethan, age fifteen, and his younger brother Austin, age ten, jumped on their four-wheelers and spent the afternoon riding the dirt trails around the foothills of the Appalachian Mountains.

Going their separate ways, their paths eventually crossed.

Police say the two brothers came around a turn on one of the trails, traveling at a decent rate of speed, when they hit head-on. Thrown from his ATV, Austin became an eighty-pound human projectile. The top of his head collided with the face of his older brother, Ethan.

Austin was knocked out, having broken his jaw, left arm, several ribs, and a few vertebrae. Even though Ethan had broken every bone in his face, he somehow remained alert enough to run for help.

Austin spent nine weeks in a coma. Ethan lost the use of his left eye and went through numerous reconstructive surgeries to repair the damage done to his face. When Austin finally woke up, his older brother carried him to and from rehabilitation appointments, and between classes in the hallway of their rural school.

When asked about the terrible nature of the accident, Ethan

said, "I feel like God shut one eye, but opened the other so I could see."[1]

Oftentimes, people who survive an episode of profound complexity come through it with a profound appreciation for the simplicity of life.

That was true for David. As the king of Israel, his life was stressful. Between governing problems and personal problems, there was nothing easy about his life. One of his outlets for dealing with the emotional weight of his problems was writing songs.

"Shout for joy to the LORD, all the earth," he wrote. "Worship the LORD with gladness; come before him with joyful songs" (Ps. 100:1–2 NIV).

I want to be able to do that, but how? How do we shout for joy when we're out of money? How do we shout for joy when the doctor says it's cancer? How do we shout for joy when everyone around us is getting married but we aren't? How do we shout for joy when everyone around us is getting pregnant but we can't?

The next lyric in David's song gives us some insight: "Know that the LORD is God. It is he who made us, and we are his" (Ps. 100:3 NIV).

He is God and we are his.

God made you. Have you ever stopped to think about how incredible you are? Your ears can identify over three hundred thousand different sounds. Your eyes can see approximately eight million different colors. And if all six hundred muscles in your body pulled in the same direction at the same time, you could lift an astounding fifty thousand pounds. There's hope for skinny guys like me!

Here's a fun idea to get lost in: your brain named itself.

The most complex part of God's creation is the human brain. And what do we use to study the brain with? The brain! Takes one to know one.

You are incredible! And if you are incredible, what does that make the Being who made you? God is the perfect balance of simplicity and complexity.

"For God so loved the world that he gave his one and only Son" (John 3:16 NIV). That's so simple a child can understand it.

"He determines the number of the stars and calls them each by name" (Ps. 147:4 NIV). That's so complex an astrophysicist can't understand it.

Simplexity.

He is God and we are his.

I live near the Red River Gorge, and there is a trail that leads to Creation Falls—one of the most beautiful places on the planet. Fish swim in the pool below it, and birds fly in the sky above it. It is a waterfall that washes away the worries of my life and carries me to the feet of my Creator.

I believe God created us to be outside, and one of the reasons we have more sadness than gladness is because we spend the majority of our lives inside.

I was at my son's soccer game a few weeks ago, sitting on the sidelines with other parents and families. We were surrounded by beautiful maple and oak trees that reached for heaven and whose leaves sang when the wind rustled them.

At halftime, I saw a woman walking across the field and drinking from a plastic water bottle. When she finished drinking it, instead of throwing it in a trash can, she chucked it on the field. Everyone around me saw it. Everyone looked stunned.

I jumped up out of my chair, ran onto the field, and picked it up. Then I chased her down, tapped her on the shoulder, and with a big smile on my face, I said, "Ma'am, I saw you drop this. I didn't want you to get to your car without it, so I thought I would bring it to you!"

She turned as white as a ghost! I said, "You're welcome," as I handed it back to her.

Everyone on the sidelines applauded for me as I returned to my seat. My wife said, "You are becoming your dad!"

Whether it's his people or his planet, I love God's creation too much to see it disrespected. And what I've learned from spending time at Creation Falls is this: The more time I spend outside with God, the more I understand what is happening inside of me. It's a beautiful exchange of sadness for gladness, complexity for simplicity.

"Though the fig tree does not bud and there are no grapes on the vines, though the olive crop fails and the fields produce no food, though there are no sheep in the pen and no cattle in the stalls," Habakkuk wrote, "yet I will rejoice in the Lord, I will be joyful in God my Savior" (Hab. 3:17–18 NIV).

Disappointment reveals a lot about us. It primarily reveals who or what we've put our faith in. Disappointment might be the greatest indicator of idolatry in our lives. People are going to let us down. Life is going to let us down. But God never will.

"For the Lord is good and his love endures forever" (Ps. 100:5 NIV).

David wanted us to know that we are God's, and God is good. I don't make T-shirts or bumper stickers, but if I did, that would be a great phrase to mass-produce.

He is God. We are his. He is good.

David knew one of the best ways to deal with the complexities of life is to sing. Singing allows God to take the pressure we feel building up inside of us and pull it outside. Singing allows us in whatever posture we want to assume—hands raised in desperation, face to the ground in utter fatigue—to express in the presence of others who are also holding on by a thread that he is God, we are his, and he is good.

Louisa Stead went on vacation with her husband and daughter. Lying on the beach, they heard the desperate cries of a young boy who was drowning just offshore. Mr. Stead quickly made his way into the water to save the boy, but soon learned it wasn't going to be an easy task.

The boy, who was scared, struggled with Mr. Stead. In a moment of panic, the two of them lost their ability to stay afloat. Mrs. Stead and her daughter watched this horrific scene unfolding, unable to do anything about it.

Louisa Stead lost her husband and was left with the daunting task of raising her daughter on her own. In the midst of it, she did what David did: she wrote a song.

> 'Tis so sweet to trust in Jesus, just to take him at his word; just to rest upon his promise, just to know, "Thus saith the Lord." Jesus, Jesus, how I trust him! How I've proved him o'er and o'er! Jesus, Jesus, precious Jesus! O for grace to trust him more![2]

We don't sing to God because life is good. We sing to God because God is good. The more pain we have, the more we need to sing. Singing helps us trust God when we don't feel like trusting God. It helps us see him when we can't see him.

J. Vernon McGee once wrote, "This is God's universe, and He is doing things His way. You may think you have a better way, but you don't have a universe to rule."[3]

Close one eye to the problem you are facing and focus your open eye on God. Big problems become small when you are looking at a big God.

18

ABSURDITY: BOTHER HIM

I HAVE A FRIEND, AND HIS NAME IS B.

It's not a nickname or an abbreviation. His legal name is B.

His daughter Laney and my daughter Ava are best friends. When the girls were in the third grade, their class took a field trip to the fort Daniel Boone built and protected in the formative years of our country's development.

B and I signed up to drive our daughters and their friends. We were the only dads on the trip, so we decided to make our car the fun car to ride in. We stopped at a gas station to buy some candy, which caused us to get lost from the rest of the caravan.

Being men, we didn't stop to ask for directions, and eventually one of the teachers called to ask where we were. B answered the phone and his explanation was one for the ages.

"We had to stop at a gas station and buy Jon Weece some cigarettes," B told her as my eyes got big! "Jon gets the shakes if he doesn't have a smoke break every hour."

As the girls in our car laughed, I shook my head in disbelief.

When we finally arrived at the fort, the teacher shot me a disappointed look and the moms of other kids gave me the cold shoulder. I am a pastor by profession, and there was no way for me to regain my dignity.

Meanwhile, B watched all of it unfold with a smile on his face.

I felt desperate because I couldn't undo what had been done.

Ever felt desperate? Ever been in a situation in life when you were totally and completely helpless and you didn't know what to do or who to turn to?

I have a friend whose son was murdered. The son stood up for a boy who was being picked on by a group of bullies, and the bullies killed him for standing up for the weaker kid. The bullies were from families that were politically well-connected, and no charges were filed against them. It was one of the most difficult funerals I've ever had to preach because the room was filled with anger and confusion and pain.

Friends and family members were desperate. They didn't know what to do with what they were feeling.

"We trust Jesus," were the words I heard the mom say over and over again. "Only Jesus can help us get through this."

Jesus was approached by a dad whose daughter was sick and needed help. The dad's name was Jairus, and like me, he was a preacher.

Jairus came and fell down before Jesus, pleading with him to heal his daughter. "My little daughter is dying," he said in desperation. "Please come and lay your hands on her; heal her so she can live" (Mark 5:22 NLT).

I recently walked into the home of a family whose college-age daughter had taken her life. Pain and shock don't even begin to describe the emotional climate of that moment. It was sheer desperation. One family member hyperventilated and passed out upon receiving the news.

That family didn't need me. They needed Jesus. They needed a power greater and bigger and stronger than themselves.

That's why I love this little line in Jairus's story: "Jesus went with him" (Mark 5:24 NLT).

In the same way that Jesus walked with Jairus, he will walk with the family in our church who lost their daughter. He will walk with you too. It doesn't matter if Jesus is your first option or your last option; if you want help, Jesus wants to help you.

I keep a picture of a seven-year-old girl with cancer in my prayer journal. The photo won a prestigious award for photography a few years ago. The picture shows her looking in the mirror, and in her reflection she has drawn a head of hair. The radiation and chemo that robbed her of her beautiful hair were replaced by a vivid imagination, and an equally avid hope that her hair would soon return.

I keep it where I can see it because it reminds me that all of us need help. All of us have something in our lives that we wish we could change. All of us have a challenge requiring a power greater than our own. But all too often we're afraid to ask for help because we're afraid to admit that we need help.

As Jesus walked with Jairus to his house, some friends of Jairus showed up and let him know that his daughter had died.

"Why bother the teacher anymore?" they said (Mark 5:35 NIV).

Why bother?

Have you ever thought that?

I'm so out of shape, why bother eating right and exercising now? My marriage is so far gone, why bother going to counseling now? I am so far in debt, why bother putting a budget in place now?

Or students, maybe you're thinking, *Why bother staying pure when all my friends are messing around sexually and making fun of me for guarding my virginity?*

Why bother?

I have some friends whose two-year-old daughter, Olivia, has an inoperable brain tumor. They were recently told there was nothing medical science could do for her. They sent her home to die. I talked with Olivia's dad about the decision.

"Her life with Jesus really will be better than her life with us," he said over the phone. "But that doesn't make it any easier to accept that we won't get to see her grow up."

As a dad, my heart broke when I heard that.

Olivia's dad was tired, so I decided to bother Jesus on his behalf. And here's why: Jesus ignored their comments and said to Jairus, "Don't be afraid. Just have faith" (Mark 5:36 NLT).

Sometimes we need to follow Jesus' example and ignore the doubts of those around us. Jesus can do things that no one else can do, but that is hard to believe when pain surrounds us on all sides. It's also hard to believe because we're surrounded by other people who can also do amazing things.

Wim Hof is from the Netherlands, and he climbed nearly to the top of Mount Everest wearing nothing but shorts and boots. He didn't have a coat or a hat or gloves. Mr. Hof figured out how to regulate his body temperature, so it's no surprise that he can do what he does.

Alain Robert is from France, and he climbs the tallest buildings in the world without the aid of a harness or a rope. He studied natural climbers like monkeys and squirrels and uses their techniques to scale the exteriors of skyscrapers, so it's no surprise that he can do what he does.

Dean Karnazes is from the United States, and he completed fifty marathons, one in each state, over the course of fifty days. I can't run to the mailbox and back without needing an Advil and some oxygen!

Jesus walked into the bedroom of a little girl who was dead and did something that no one else in the course of human history has ever been able to do.

"Holding her hand, he said to her, 'Talitha koum,' which means 'Little girl, get up!' And the girl, who was twelve years old, immediately stood up and walked around!" (Mark 5:41–42 NLT).

Climbing a mountain in shorts is one thing. Raising someone from the dead defies all explanation. Jesus is in a category all to himself, and that's exactly why we need to bother him. It's why we need to tap him on the shoulder and ask for help. It's why we need to put our faith in him.

Faith is used as a noun 243 times in the New Testament. Faith is used as a verb 243 times in the New Testament. What does that tell us? It tells us that faith is equally about *what* we believe and what we *do* with what we believe.

If what I believe about Jesus doesn't translate into how I live, then what's the point? Belief has to affect behavior for it to be faith. Jairus believed Jesus could heal his daughter, so he asked Jesus to heal his daughter. He had nothing to lose and everything to gain by trusting Jesus to do what no one else can do.

My good friend Jud has practiced medicine for more than thirty years, and he said the legal definition for death is the cessation of all brain function, which is irreversible.

The key word is *irreversible*. What makes everything that we consider impossible to be possible with Jesus is his ability to reverse the irreversible.

And I haven't mentioned it yet, but on the way to raise this twelve-year-old girl from the dead, Jesus healed a woman who had been bleeding for twelve years. One woman's blood stopped, but another woman's bleeding wouldn't stop. One was rich and one was poor. One had everything to lose and the other had nothing to lose. What Mark is trying to help us see by comparing and contrasting these two women is that Jesus doesn't discriminate. Educated or uneducated, rich or poor, young or old, male or female—all Jesus sees when he looks at us is our need, and what he wants us to see when we look at him is his ability to meet that need.

Jesus can do what no one else can do.

Augustine once said, "Miracles are not in contradiction to nature. They are only in contradiction with what we know of nature." Jesus not only created the natural world we live in. He also controls it.

In the natural world, people want to limit conversations to facts. The fact is this little girl was dead. But another equally valid fact is that Jesus raised her from the dead. He also raised himself from the dead.

So what do we do with Jesus? Seriously, what do we do with someone like Jesus who seems to be a self-contained source of unlimited power?

I think there's only one thing to do.

Trust him.

I remember praying for my dad to be healed from cancer, and I remember the moment he died. My oldest brother said, "God answered our prayers." Though I wanted to keep my dad around, I knew the greater miracle wasn't the fact that God could heal him of cancer, but that God could raise him from the dead.

So I'm doing what I did before my dad died.

I'm trusting Jesus.

One of the reasons I trust Jesus is because of what he did for the little girl *after* he raised her from the dead: "He told them to give her something to eat" (Mark 5:43 NLT).

Being dead will make you hungry.

What this little detail in the narrative tells me is that Jesus really cared about her. Her growling stomach mattered as much to him as her beating heart. And when everyone tried to direct all the attention toward Jesus, he immediately redirected it toward the little girl. I'm drawn to his humility as much as I am his power, and it makes me trust him and love him even more.

If you've reached a point of desperation in your life, can I encourage you to trust Jesus? If you feel as though you're facing something that is impossible to get past, can I encourage you to trust Jesus? If you've said "Why bother?" in recent weeks, can I encourage you to trust Jesus enough to bother him?

Tap him on the shoulder and ask for help.

19

PRIORITY: INTERROBANG

WHEN MY SON WAS FIVE, HE CAME HOME FROM SCHOOL WITH A NOTE FROM his teacher that said, "Silas needs to work on not saying the word *wiener* so often in class!"

Nothing makes a dad prouder and a mom angrier than a boy who finds it funny to talk about wieners.

As I read over the note again, I noticed the punctuation at the end of the teacher's sentence. She finished the sentence with an exclamation mark.

Old typewriters used to have a key for a punctuation mark we don't use anymore called the interrobang.

It's an exclamation point and a question mark all in one.

It looks like this:

$$‽$$

Someday God will put an exclamation point where we've had a question mark. The Bible refers to it as the *Parousia*. We know it as the Second Coming.

My buddy John had a hard marriage; then his wife left him for a career. In the wake of it, living on a farm with his black labrador, he learned to be content as a single man. But nothing about it was easy. The grief was suffocating at times.

And that's when God led a beautiful, single mom into his life. In a matter of months, John's life radically changed. He married Alecia and they added a son to the mix.

"Are you happy?" John asked his stepdaughter over bowls of cereal.

"Yes, I am," she said between bites.

"Why are you happy?" John continued.

"Because of my bunk bed, my swing set, and eating together as a family!" she answered with excitement.

ME TOO

John would tell you that God hasn't connected all the dots for him yet. But the question marks are fading, and they're being replaced with exclamations about bunk beds and swing sets and eating together as a family.

God has a unique way of straightening out the curve in question marks.

There's coming a day when everything will be straightened out. Jesus came and Jesus is coming. The second time will be different than the first time. The first time he came, he didn't stay. The second time he comes, he will stay.

Forever.

Earth is his home. We're just squatters who have done a terrible job of taking care of his property. We've vandalized more than just our hearts; we've polluted his planet with our toxic behavior.

That's why he has to destroy earth and re-create it. That makes sense to me. I don't want to spend eternity living in a place like the one I'm currently living in. Don't get me wrong: I love Kentucky and all the green grass and rolling hills and horse farms. It's what is unseen that disturbs me. It's the hidden darkness in people's hearts, my own included, that I'm ready for Jesus to throw on the biggest bonfire the universe has ever seen. There is a genuine ache, a genuine pain in my heart for things to be better than they are.

PRIORITY: INTERROBANG

We don't let our children use the word *hate* in our home. But I can tell you, there are things about this world that I hate.

I hate violence.

I hate racism.

I hate child abuse.

I hate addiction.

I hate war.

I hate starvation.

I hate disease.

What bothers me about this world bothers God even more.

But good can come from bad. God turned the ugliness of the cross into a spectacle of eternal beauty. And he will do the same with the pain of this world.

Barbara Brown Taylor spent years living in the woods, asking God to teach her about darkness.

"Sitting deep in the heart of Organ Cave," she wrote, "I let this sink in: new life starts in the dark. Whether it is a seed in the ground, a baby in the womb, or Jesus in the tomb, it starts in the dark."[1]

ME TOO

I shared that with a young woman who had been sold into prostitution by her stepdad and older brother. They pimped her out to businessmen and tourists. When I met her, she was a fragile shell of a person. She attempted suicide multiple times because the pain she endured was overwhelming.

God restored the years the locusts had eaten.

But there is still residue. There is still a faint memory of the trauma and the damage men inflicted on her. And that won't go away until Jesus returns.

But it *will* go away.

20

ETERNITY: THE
ALREADY NOT YET

THERE IS A BOOK ENTITLED *LAST WORDS OF NOTABLE PEOPLE*, AND IT records the final words of people prior to dying. Beloved news anchor Tim Russert said, "What's happening?" before taking his last breath. Thomas Edison said, "It is very beautiful over there," as he looked out a window. The famous last words of a Civil War general by the name of Sedgwick? "They couldn't hit an elephant at this distance."[1]

And most rednecks die saying, "Hey, watch this!"

Have you ever been in an argument with your spouse, and in the heat of the battle he or she says, "Honey, you can have the last word"? Rare if ever!

The last recorded words of Jesus were, "Yes, I am coming soon" (Rev. 22:20 NIV). And they aren't just the last words of Jesus. They're some of the last words of the Bible. And interestingly, they're couched in marriage terminology.

After our honeymoon, Allison and I were driving back to Lexington when we had our first fight. I don't remember what we disagreed about, but I do remember she was so mad she didn't talk to me for thirty minutes.

The dreaded silent treatment!

As we passed a farm, I noticed that she was looking at a few donkeys in a field near a barn. So I asked, "Relatives of yours?"

There was a long pause, and then my wife said, "Yes, by marriage!"

In fifteen years of marriage, I've never won an argument.

According to the book of Revelation, instead of being rescued from a marriage, we will be rescued by a marriage: "I saw the Holy City, the new Jerusalem, coming down out of heaven from God, prepared as a bride beautifully dressed for her husband" (21:2 NIV).

And when you think about this wedding day between Jesus (the groom) and his bride (the church), I don't want you to think "solemn and somber" as much as I want you to think "festive and fun." The party to end all parties!

Jesus will reverse the curse. What happened in Genesis 1–2 is undone in Revelation 21–22. Four times in Revelation 21 God uses the word *new* to describe what is waiting for us on our wedding day.

"He who was seated on the throne said, 'I am making everything *new!*'" (Rev. 21:5 NIV, emphasis mine).

The Greek word John uses for *new* is *kainos*. *Kainos* is not the common word used in the New Testament for *new*, which is *neos*. *Neos* is when you take an old car and overhaul it and restore it. Or when you take an antique piece of furniture and refurbish it and say, "Just like new!"

Kainos represents something completely and comprehensively new, totally new, brand-new! And *kainos* is used in 2 Corinthians 5:17 where Paul wrote, "Therefore, if anyone is in Christ, the *new* creation has come: The old has gone, the *new* is here!" (NIV, emphasis mine).

He is describing you and me. The new creation has already begun. This is why theologians refer to God's plan of redeeming all that is fallen in the universe as "the already and the not yet."

The curse has been reversed, is being reversed, and will someday be reversed. We define this reality with a four-letter word known as *hope*.

In his book *Surprised by Hope*, N. T. Wright wrote, "Easter was when Hope in person surprised the whole world by coming forward from the future into the present."[2]

The mission of the church is to bring the future into the present.

Every church is an ever-expanding outpost and colony of heaven. At the church where I serve, we want the architect of heaven to have to redesign the city to prepare for the number of people we plan on bringing with us!

You are God's commercial, God's cameo of what is and what is to come; you are the poster child of the already and the not yet.

Years ago, when Christians built a church, they would put the cemetery in the front yard. Every Sunday when they gathered, they were reminded that we have to walk through death to get to the new life.

One life at a time, we are bringing the future into the present.

To return to N. T. Wright, he articulated it this way in his book *Simply Christian:*

> "Resurrection" doesn't mean "going to heaven when you
> die" . . . It is certainly not about keeping the commands
> of a distant deity. Rather, it is the new way of being
> human, the Jesus-shaped way of being human, the
> cross-and-resurrection way of life, the Spirit-led pathway.
> It is the way which anticipates, in the present, the full,
> rich, glad human existence, which will one day be ours
> when God makes all things new. Christian ethics is not
> a matter of discovering what's going on in the world
> and getting in tune with it. It isn't a matter of doing

things to earn God's favor. It is not about trying to obey
dusty rulebooks from long ago or far away. It is about
practicing, in the present, the tunes we shall sing in God's
new world.[3]

My good friend Garrett has endured thirty-seven surgeries in the
last twenty years. Doctors have replaced everything they can
replace that is broken. His body has deteriorated but hasn't died.
He is in constant pain, but at the same time, he is a constant
source of joy for everyone he meets. He doesn't feel sorry for
himself. He doesn't beg for sympathy. He knows his current
body is not his permanent body. Someday God will give him a
new body.

And that's why instead of describing heaven as a place, John
described it as a people. The place is the people.

In Revelation, John didn't get caught up in describing the color
of the wallpaper and carpet. John described heaven using
the number twelve, which is used elsewhere in Revelation to
describe the people of God. This new city will have twelve gates
and twelve foundations. It will be 12,000 stadia, by 12,000 stadia,
by 12,000 stadia in dimension. Everywhere you look at John's
description of the city, you see the number twelve, which means
every time you see heaven, you see the people of God.

I finished mowing my yard last Friday and was in a hurry to get
to Silas's baseball practice, so I decided to change my clothes
in the garage. There aren't any houses next to us, so I didn't
think anyone would see me. As I took off my grass-covered

pants and T-shirt, I looked up and saw the UPS deliveryman standing in my driveway. He set the package down and said, "Looks like I caught you with your pants down!" He laughed and walked away.

The quickest way isn't always the best way.

Even though my friend Garrett and so many other people who are struggling and suffering in this life want Jesus to come quickly, God continues to delay his return for a reason. And God's reason for delaying the return of Jesus has something to do with wanting as many people to be ready for his return as possible.

"The Lord is not slow in keeping his promise, as some understand slowness. Instead he is patient with you, not wanting anyone to perish, but everyone to come to repentance" (2 Pet. 3:9 NIV).

Fifteen years ago I spoke at a funeral for a college cheerleader who was killed while driving under the influence of alcohol. He was the fifth college student from the same small town to die while drinking and driving.

I honored his parents' wishes by talking about the good parts of his life, and I took the opportunity to kindly invite students to think about their choices and the consequences of their actions.

After that one funeral, dozens of students surrendered their lives to Jesus, and I've had the privilege of watching many of them grow up and become active members in our church family.

From the worst of situations, God sometimes does his best work. That was true of the cross, and it can be true of your life too.

Paul wrote, "I consider that our present sufferings are not worth comparing with the glory that will be revealed in us" (Rom. 8:18 NIV). Paul was a man familiar with suffering. He had been shipwrecked, beaten, flogged, and stoned on more than one occasion.

So think about your deepest hurt, your greatest loss, the place in your heart that is most breakable and broken, and know that you can trust God right now. You can wake up tomorrow and trust his promise and know beyond a shadow of a doubt that it will be worth it in the end because he really will wipe every tear from your eyes.

A young man named William, born blind, recently became engaged to a woman who loved him in spite of his inability to see. Prior to their wedding day he went through an experimental surgery wherein doctors attempted to restore his sight. On the day of his wedding, as he stood in front of a crowd of friends and family, the doctors removed his bandages, and the first person he wanted to see was his bride.

As he struggled to focus, she eventually came into view. He said to her, "You are even more beautiful than I could have imagined."[4]

There is coming a day when we will see fully—when our vision will no longer be blinded by the pain of this world, and we will see our groom face-to-face. I promise you: that sight will be better than we can even begin to imagine!

From conversations I've had with people over the years, I think some people worry that heaven is going to be boring. They think heaven is going to be like a retirement village in Florida where we eat early and spend our afternoons playing shuffleboard and bingo!

Other people think all we're going to do in heaven is sit on clouds and sing. After some of the church services I've endured in my life, I'm convinced that eternal congregational singing may in fact be what happens in the other place!

Though worship will be incredible in heaven, I think the best way to come to an understanding of how we will spend our time and what we will do for eternity is to reflect on the parable Jesus told in Matthew 25 about the Master who gave his workers a task. He left, then came back and said, "Well done, good and faithful servant! You have been faithful with a few things; I will put you in charge of many things. Come and share your master's happiness!" (v. 23 NIV).

In the book of Genesis we learn that we were created in the image of God, and that we were created to rule and reign with God over all of creation for eternity. That's what made God happy, and it's what will make him happy again.

When Jesus comes back, time will no longer work against us. It will work for us. I was eating a banana the other day and it had a brown spot on it, but fruit will never spoil or rot. Fruit will taste increasingly better as more time elapses. Flowers won't ever wither and die; they will get more beautiful and more radiant as time passes. Relationships and conversations will get better and better because we will get better and better. Everything will be moving in the constant direction of improvement.

When Jesus comes back, the God-image in you will be fully restored. God is creative, so you will have godlike creative capacities. In heaven, the best stand-up comedy is yet to be performed, the most luxurious resorts are yet to be constructed, and the best movies are yet to be scripted! You will be able to do what you love most here on earth, like eating the best food ever prepared. I believe heaven will be one big, "Oh, you've got to try this!"

If you have a sweet tooth, you will love the chocolate in heaven, and ice cream lovers—get ready! You think Baskin-Robbins has a lot of flavors? No more cholesterol, no more counting calories!

You will get to explore every square inch of every ecosystem that is untamed and untainted—from mountains, rivers, and oceans to rain forests. You will experience the best of winter without feeling cold, and the best of summer without sweating. If you are a city person, the streets are made of gold.

What is valued here is only worth walking on there.

In this *kainos* city, void of traffic jams and crime, you will have unrestricted access to the best plays, the best art exhibits, the best museums, and the best libraries—and there won't be any lines! Concerts will never sell out, and our minds will never stop learning new things.

Dallas Willard wrote, "You will know fullness of function, the unending creativity involved in a cosmos-wide cooperative pursuit of a created order that continuously approaches but never reaches the limitless goodness of the triune personality of God."[5]

Never again will you feel as though you've wasted a day!

It's an age-old question: "Who is more content? The man with a million dollars, or the man with eight children?" The answer is, "The man with eight children because he doesn't want any more!"

Each of us has a void in us. And each of us goes about filling that shortage with something. Money, food, clothing, cars, houses, vacations, and sex are momentarily filling because they leave us wanting more. In heaven every craving, every need you have will be met because God will be there. God will occupy every square inch of the new world and preoccupy every square inch of your mind.

In our culture, people drive across the country to see the Grand Canyon or Niagara Falls. The drive takes days, but experiencing the event may last for a few hours. People will brave the elements and wait in line all day to see a movie or purchase an iPhone. People will spend excessive amounts of money to attend the Super Bowl or the Final Four.

There is coming a day when people will see God. And this is not something you do in five minutes! This is not something you finish, move on from, and say, "Hey, have you seen God yet?" as though he's just another ride at Disneyland.

It would take us millions of years, if not more, just to explore the known universe, and the scriptures teach that God holds all of it in his hands. Think about what it will be like to explore the infinite and limitless God.

John said you will see his face. You will see the face of God! You!

It's not as though you will see him passing by on a float in a parade as he waves to the masses. No, the wording used here indicates you will have a personal audience with him. You will talk with and be loved by God! You! Yes, you!

"It is the glory of God to conceal a matter; to search out a matter is the glory of kings" (Prov. 25:2 NIV).

We are co-heirs of an eternal inheritance, and we will explore and experience God in all the vastness and volume of his eternal being.

On Monday I received one of those phone calls in life that stops you dead in your tracks. One of my good friends, a former coworker of mine in Haiti, called to let me know that his four-year-old son had just been diagnosed with leukemia.

As I started to pray, I sensed the Spirit of God saying to me, "Jon,

instead of praying for him, why don't you go and pray with him?"
So I grabbed a toothbrush and my cell phone, and I turned my
car toward Springfield, Illinois.

My friend's son reminded me so much of my own son. And when I
learned that little Nate was facing three years of chemotherapy,
the tears came and my thoughts again turned to the reality of
heaven.

I don't know about you, but I need heaven.

It is more than an occupational need. I need heaven on a very
personal level. And what makes it heaven for me is the God who
lives there—the God whose love will finally fulfill every longing of
my being.

The God who doesn't want another child like Nate to suffer
another minute of another day.

"Yes, I am coming soon."

END HERE—REST FOR ALL OF US

ONE WEEKEND AT OUR CHURCH WE GAVE EVERYONE A BASEBALL-SIZED balloon filled with paint. We placed giant canvases in each parking lot, and we encouraged everyone to throw the balloon as a way of unloading whatever tension they had inside of them. Young and old, right-handed and left-handed, they lined up and didn't hold back.

They let go.

They took aim—throwing hurt and anger and pain and bitterness—and it did more than create the messy graphic used on the cover of this book. It united our church family around our common struggle and around our Father's ability to replace frustration with freedom.

I stood at a distance and watched as people walked away. They seemed lighter. They seem relieved.

They seemed rested.

I recently read about a Great Dane that wasn't feeling well. His owner took him to the veterinarian, and after an X-ray, everyone realized why the massive dog wasn't feeling well. Something was stuffed in the dog's stomach. And after a two-hour surgery, everyone knew what that something was.

Forty-three socks.

When folding laundry, I sometimes have a sock that is missing its partner. I'm confident that if I were missing forty-three socks, I would begin to ask some questions.

We all have stuff inside of us that leaves us feeling crummy. Someday all of the bad experiences and bad emotions that we've been carrying around will be released from our hearts for good.

Everyone will be able to take a deep breath.

Everyone will be able to rest.

C. S. Lewis ended his classic series, The Chronicles of Narnia, with these words:

> The things that began to happen after that were so great and beautiful that I cannot write them. And for us this is the end of all the stories, and we can most truly say that they all lived happily ever after. But for them it was only the beginning of the real story. All their life in this world . . . had only been the cover and the title page: now at last they were beginning Chapter One of the Great Story,

which no one on earth has read, which goes on for ever: in which every chapter is better than the one before.[1]

Your story is just beginning. Do not allow your life to be defined by the title page. There is a better story playing out, so don't settle for a role in the drama this world is writing. Instead, insert yourself into God's sentence, and look forward to the day when he writes, "The end is really the beginning."

ACKNOWLEDGMENTS

ALLISON—THIS BOOK BEGAN IN 1997 ON A PLAYGROUND IN HAITI WHEN you trusted me with the details of your story. You continue to teach me that intimacy flows from vulnerability. Because of that, I feel safe when I'm with you.

Kim Pascual—This book would not be a reality without your administrative support and encouragement. Thanks for going the extra mile on the editing front.

Chris Hahn—You are an incredible leader and an even better friend. I can close my office door with confidence because I know the church is in good hands. Thanks for freeing me up to write.

The Elders at Southland—Creating a church culture with you where struggling people can be enveloped by the grace of God has been one of the highlights of my life. Heaven will reveal that the risks we've taken were worth it.

ACKNOWLEDGMENTS

The Southland Family—You embody the message of this book better than any group of people I know. Like God, your love for people is wide, long, high, and deep.

Don Gates—Thanks for believing in me and going to bat for me. Your partnership in ministry is a gift that I greatly appreciate.

Jocelyn Bailey, Katherine Rowley, Kristin Parrish, and Brian Hampton—You bring a rare combination of expertise and humility to the table. Working with you has been a joy and a privilege.

NOTES

BEGIN HERE—ALL OF US ARE LIKE THE REST OF US
1. C. S. Lewis, *The Four Loves* (Orlando: Harcourt, 1960), 78.

CHAPTER 1—VULNERABILITY: A THREE-LEGGED RACE
1. Robert D. Putnam, *Bowling Alone* (New York: Simon & Schuster, 2000), 331–332.
2. Millard J. Erickson, *Christian Theology*, 2nd ed. (Grand Rapids: Baker, 1998), 751.

CHAPTER 2—ACCESSIBILITY: LUCILLE
1. Joachim Jeremias, *The Prayers of Jesus* (New York: SCM Press, 1967), 57, as quoted in Max Lucado, *The Great House of God* (Nashville: Thomas Nelson, 1997) 13–14.
2. Associated Press, "Girl Talks About Imminent Death After Her Siamese Twin Sister Dies," *New York Times*, July 22, 1991, www.nytimes.com/1991/07/22/us/girl-talks-about-imminent-death-after-her-siamese-twin-sister-dies.html.
3. Michael Finkel, "The Strange and Curious Tale of the Last True Hermit," accessed July 8, 2015, http://www.gq.com/news-politics/newsmakers/201409/the-last-true-hermit.

NOTES

CHAPTER 3—ABILITY: GIVE ME YOUR LUNCH MONEY
1. Used with permission, http://jesserice.com.

CHAPTER 5—IDENTITY: YOU, ME, AND E.T.
1. Calvin Miller, *The Singer: A Classic Retelling of Cosmic Conflict* (Downers Grove, IL: InterVarsity, 2001), 5.
2. P. T. Forsyth, as quoted in Matt Proctor, *Victorious: A Devotional Study of Revelation* (Joplin, MO: College Press, 2013), 84.
3. G. K. Chesterton, *Orthodoxy* (Mineola, NY: Dover, 2004), 52.

CHAPTER 6—HUMILITY: *KINTSUGI*
1. Heard by the author in a sermon by Pete Wilson a few years ago.
2. John Ortberg, *The Life You've Always Wanted: Spiritual Disciplines for Ordinary People* (Grand Rapids, MI: Zondervan, 2002), 86.
3. William MacDonald, *Lord, Break Me!* (Kansas City: Walterick, 1972), 4.

CHAPTER 8—INCLUSIVITY: FROM CRUMBS TO COMMUNION
1. John Newton, "Amazing Grace," 1779, v. 7 by Anonymous /Unknown, pub. 1829.

CHAPTER 9—OPPORTUNITY: A DAD WHO UNDERSTANDS MOMS
1. See www.save.org and www.jasonfoundation.org.
2. Jamie Tworkowski, "There Is Still Some Time," *To Write Love On Her Arms* (blog), August 11, 2014, http://twloha.com/blog /there-still-some-time/.

CHAPTER 10—INTEGRITY: CROOKED LINES
1. Isaac Watts, "At the Cross," 1707, ref. by Ralph E. Hudson, 1885.
2. Joel B. Green, *The Gospel of Luke* (Grand Rapids: Wm. B. Eerdmans, 1997), 310.

3. Frank Viola, "John Lennon on Jesus: The Untold Story," *Patheos*, July 8, 2013, http://www.patheos.com/blogs/frankviola /johnlennononjesus/.

CHAPTER 13—AVAILABILITY: TRAPPED ON A PLANE WITH A SKUNK

1. Darabont, Frank, Niki Marvin, Tim Robbins, Morgan Freeman, Bob Gunton, William Sadler, Clancy Brown, et al., *The Shawshank Redemption* (Burbank, CA: Warner Bros. Pictures, 2004), DVD.

CHAPTER 14—UNITY: GOOD DONUTS, BAD THEOLOGY

1. Max Lucado, as quoted in Charles R. Swindoll, *The Tale of the Tardy Oxcart* (Nashville: Thomas Nelson, 1998), 338.
2. Charles R. Swindoll, *The Grace Awakening* (Nashville: Thomas Nelson, 2010), 1–2.

CHAPTER 16—SENSITIVITY: FLIGHT 5191

1. Mark Barry, "The Lawn Chair Pilot," accessed June 24, 2015, www.markbarry.com/lawnchairman.html.

CHAPTER 17—RELIABILITY: SIMPLEXITY

1. Cassondra Kirby, "Bond of Brothers: Wreck Shows Boys How Much They Mean to Each Other," *Lexington Herald-Leader*, February 15, 2006.
2. Kenneth W. Osbeck, *Amazing Grace: 366 Inspiring Hymn Stories for Daily Devotions* (Grand Rapids: Kregel Publications, 2010), 220.
3. J. Vernon McGee, *Thru the Bible: 1 Corinthians Through Revelation* (Nashville: Thomas Nelson, 1983), 236.

CHAPTER 19—PRIORITY: INTERROBANG

1. Barbara Brown Taylor, *Learning to Walk in the Dark* (New York: HarperOne, 2014), 129.

NOTES

CHAPTER 20—ETERNITY: THE ALREADY NOT YET

1. Thomas Edison, as quoted in William B. Brahms, *Last Words of Notable People* (Haddonfield, NJ: Reference Desk Press, 2010).
2. N. T. Wright, *Surprised by Hope: Rethinking Heaven, the Resurrection, and the Mission of the Church* (New York: HarperOne, 2008), 29.
3. N. T. Wright, *Simply Christian: Why Christianity Makes Sense* (New York: HarperOne, 2006), 218, 222.
4. Kent Crockett, "Heaven," *KentCrockett.com* (blog), accessed July 8, 2015, http://www.kentcrockett.com/cgi-bin/illustrations/index.cgi?topic=Heaven.
5. Dallas Willard, as quoted in John Ortberg, *Revelation: Experience God's Power* (Grand Rapids: Zondervan, 2002), 58.

END HERE—REST FOR ALL OF US

1. C. S. Lewis, *The Last Battle* (New York: HarperCollins, 1956), 228.

ABOUT THE AUTHOR

JON WEECE IS THE LEAD PASTOR AT SOUTHLAND CHRISTIAN CHURCH, A community of 14,000 Christ-followers in Lexington, Kentucky. He is the author of *Jesus Prom*. Prior to Southland, Jon was a missionary to Haiti for four years, where he met his wife, Alli. They have two children.